A BRUSH WITH JEFF

and Other Essays

For more information, address: turftavernpress@gmail.com

First paperback edition December 2024
Book design and Illustrations by Nuno Moreira, NMDESIGN
ISBN 978-1-7347445-2-1 (Paperback)
ISBN 978-1-7347445-1-4 (ebook)
Printed and bound in the United States of America
First printing December 2024
jechadwick.com

A BRUSH WITH JEFF

and Other Essays

J.E. CHADWICK

To my family

&

all my forever friends.

And Jeff.

ESSAYS

A LIGHT INTRODUCTION

This is not the book I intended to write.

A *Brush With Jeff* is a book that was seduced by the idea it contained. Like an unsuspecting host gently eaten and transformed by a benign parasite, it emerged as a bright creature of indeterminate species at the last minute.

The idea I tried to write about was *lightness*. I had become obsessed with it, seeing it everywhere I looked—every movie, every artwork, every leaf and cloud—until I needed to write something down.

My obsession began with a single line by the French poet Paul Valéry:

Il faut être *léger comme l'oiseau et non comme la plume.*

Or

One should be light like a bird and not like a feather.

That line struck me as important and true. We *should* want to grow lighter with control, like a bird in flight, not like a feather buffeted by the wind. It explained the natural arc of human life: *light, heavy, light again.* We are born light, and every child should remain so as long as possible. We should be light when young, with little anxiety and great freedom. Like a feather in the wind, the universe will reveal its purpose.

Then, as young adults, we decide that we want to live a full life with all its commitments—a career, a partner, and children to raise in a beautiful home we own. We choose to pursue this full life, and it soon becomes heavy. We take on weighty responsibilities, which almost paralyze us. Often, we lose all sense of who we are and what we want, let alone how to get it.

But as we age we often shed responsibilities, and we might learn to embrace lightness again. We can become light *like a bird*, with elegant control and purpose. Waiting for the right time to shift gear, we might cut ourselves free, gently, and skillfully. We hope to create and love more and crave less; to live our next act in lightness.

This was the potent idea I had to write about.

But how? I started writing a book called *Lightness: The Gentle Art of Cutting Yourself Free*, in which each chapter tackled a different escape: free from anger, free from ego, free from anxiety, and so on. These were big, meaty questions, but I plowed on for months, solving the world's problems one freedom at a time. After a dozen chapters, I started slowing and then ground to a halt, imprisoned by a self-imposed structure, sinking into muddy prose.

My book on lightness had become irremediably heavy.

Meanwhile, my actual life was growing lighter. I retired, meditated daily, bought a camper van, and explored the American West, often disappearing off the grid. By working out and eating well, I shed fifteen pounds. I even found love and intimacy again. But most of all, during that period, I curled up in a big chair and devoured books without worrying that I should do something else more important. I had cut things from my life to create a fresh space, and the thing that filled those hours was reading books in a big chair. And in every book, I still found those same calls to lightness:

"The free soul is rare, but you know it when you see it — basically because you feel good, very good, when you are near or with them."
— Charles Bukowski

"I want to sing like the birds sing, not worrying about who hears or what they think."
— Rumi

"Sliding brings lightness; lightness brings forgetting"
— Steven Kotler on skiing, Gnar Country

"To attain knowledge, add things every day. To attain wisdom, subtract things every day."
— Lao Tzu

A genuine sense of humor is having a light touch: not beating reality into the ground but appreciating reality with a light touch. The basis of Shambhala vision is rediscovering that perfect and real sense of humor, that light touch of appreciation."
— Chögyam Trungpa, Shambhala

The urge to write returned. I reread my chapters, hoping they were better than I remembered. They were not; my writing was sometimes profound but mostly turgid. The serious soul who toiled on those essays seemed like a stranger to me now; he lacked joy, playfulness, and, well, lightness. The manuscript was worthy, but not worthy of publishing, and the prospect of a full rewrite left me nauseous.

However, the prospect of writing a fresh essay each week

excited me. The urge was simply to write, not to publish a book. I landed on the name *Like A Bird*, launched a Substack newsletter, and started publishing one essay every Wednesday morning.

Writing essays became a joy again. I kept a list of dozens of ideas, and each week, I sat down with an empty page and chose what to fill it with: the ultimate freedom. I only wrote when ambitious and playful — often just after dawn with strong, black coffee.

Part of the satisfaction of this cadence is getting feedback soon after publishing. The essay on *Luna Luna: The Greatest Art Story Ever Told* inspired several readers to buy tickets to view the exhibition in L.A. after which they shared their own experiences. In *Cooking For Forty Silent Strangers*, I described serving food for ten days at a silent retreat, after which a few signed up for a Vipassana course. An essay on *Watching One Day: Six Ways We Misunderstand Love* inspired a family member to share their own experience of love unexpectedly.

Before long, I had enough essays to consider a book again. Nothing beats a physical object; you can hold it up to your nose and smell it or gift it to a friend with a loving inscription. Forget chocolates and roses; nothing says I love you like an inscribed book.

I also wanted to work with an artist again – it's like switching on a bigger, richer backup brain. When I published my first book, *Path*, I collaborated with my son Lawrence, a professional artist in London, who sketched thirty and illustrations for the interior. The instant wonder of his sketches more than compensated for the mediocrity of my prose. I don't understand why more readers don't insist on delightful book design; even good writing improves with art.

This time, my son was too busy preparing for an exhibition, so I reached out to an artist in Lisbon whom I admire. Many of the essays had been written in Portugal, Spain, Austria and Croatia, while I'd been traveling to watch my youngest son play international football, so I was looking for a European modernist aesthetic. The manuscript I sent him — an edited selection of my favorite twenty essays — was titled *Like A Bird*, and he was excited to collaborate on it.

But something wasn't right.

The name was memorable, but ironically, it still seemed heavy. It implied a powerful ordering principle, a philosophy of lightness, that somehow shaped every essay's curves. There was an unspoken hint that if you, dear reader, should make your way through this book of essays, you might also find lightness in your life.

In short, it suggested I was selling an idea. I'm not. I'm not selling anything.

After rereading and editing, one essay was shimmering brighter than the others — *A Brush With Jeff: The Art Of Walking Around European Cities.* The essay meanders through a sunny day in Vienna with light-hearted friends and an eccentric, free-spirited local guide called Jeff. Although he's not actually Austrian. And he's not called Jeff. And when he finally leaves us, we all somehow feel different:

We know our brush with Jeff represents something special, something rare and birdlike, something missing from our daily lives, an echo of our youth, but we can't put it into words.

I realized this story belonged up front and on the cover. In describing a single, free-spirited day, I had at last written *with* lightness, without writing *about* lightness.

Writing these twenty essays changed me in unexpected ways and helped me reconnect over ideas with good friends.

But most of all they helped me find a new, lighter voice.

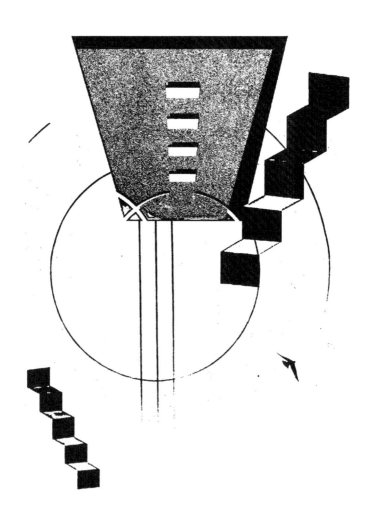

A BRUSH WITH JEFF:
THE ART OF WALKING AROUND
EUROPEAN CITIES

Years ago, when the boys were young, we used to fly from London to Austria every December to ski for a week. We'd land in Innsbruck, then hire a taxi to Mayrhofen, and they would point to the snowcapped mountains along the way and get excited. Excited boys are loud, so I'd usually make up a trivia quiz to keep them occupied and break up the journey. *Capital of Austria? Bordering countries? Most famous dish?* That sort of stuff.

—What an excellent idea! Exclaimed Nikki, our impeccably polite chauffeur. Boys, your father is clever, teaching you many facts about the world!

I liked Nikki. He deserved a tip.

—Would you be so kind as to allow me to pose some Austrian history questions of my own? He requested.

—Of course! Boys, listen to Mr. Nikki's questions. They're worth ten points each.

Nikki smiled into the rearview mirror, and then, noting a Salzburg Music Festival billboard, he landed on his first question.

—Ach so, boys, can you name the most famous Austrian of all time?

Three hands shot up in the back seat, and they chorused together:

—ADOLF HITLER!!!

After an awkward pause, Nikki awarded everyone ten points and explained that he should focus on his driving.

I tell this story over a pilsner to Jeff, our eccentrically European tour guide in Vienna. He squeals with impish delight before taking a long drag on a Gauloise and suggests we might avoid shouting Hitler in the piazza.

We are four men in our fifties—a.k.a. The Four Wieners— and we giggle conspiratorially.

I love Jeff. I love his passion for culture and history and how he has an unexpected story or trivia question for every medieval and baroque cranny of Vienna. The way he smokes and drinks his way from café to café, urging us to look up, always to look up, to see the thousands of statues on top of the palaces, castles, and townhouses. How he effortlessly threads his stories through European countries, languages, and historical eras.

He is Jeff of Europe. He is precisely what we came for.

And yet, I almost canceled our tour with Jeff before it started. Twice.

First, when we arrived late at the hotel, Bernhard, the chubby receptionist, gave us a note.

—You have a message from Jeff Thomas, who is your guide for tomorrow, perhaps? He asks you to call or WhatsApp him at this number.

—Jeff Thomas? That doesn't sound very Austrian. Did you speak in German?

—He spoke in English. I would suspect he was Canadian or perhaps American.

My heart sank, which Bernhard seemed to enjoy. (What's

German for schadenfreude?) We had driven over from Croatia and only had one day to see Vienna, so we'd decided to experiment with a different kind of tour: *Vienna with a Local.* The idea was that a resident would give us a three-hour private walking tour and share insights and experiences about living in Austria. It was made very clear: This would not be with an official guide, and we could not expect our host to know every date and fact.

Our expectations had been set low, but we at least hoped to meet an authentic Viennese.

—Shall we cancel? I ask my friends.

We are too tired to decide anything, so I WhatsApp Jeff to meet us at the lobby at 9, and we crash.

In the morning, Jeff calls to suggest we meet at the cathedral instead.

—Jeff, you don't sound Austrian. Where are you from?

—Can you guess? He giggles.

—No idea

—I'm French! But of course, I live in Vienna and am passionate about the city.

—OK Jeff, we'll see you at nine at the cathedral. À bientôt.

—À bientôt.

An hour later, at nine, we are outside the cathedral, and Jeff texts to say he's running late.

—Shall we cancel? I ask again. I feel responsible.

We decide to wait. We're in too deep, and more than a little curious.

Jeff finally shuffles up and introduces himself. He wears ripped jeans, dirty sneakers, and a teenage shoulder bag, and offers a yellow-stained smoker's handshake. Aged anywhere between thirty and seventy, Jeff is scrawny and rakishly European good-looking, as if David Bowie kept on a lovable but naughty twin brother as a roadie who could never be fired.

Selfishly, as a Brit traveling with two well-dentured Americans, I'm relieved that his teeth are worse than mine, but his smile is so wildly infectious that it doesn't seem to offend them.

Vienna is perhaps the world's greatest walking city, a giant UNESCO World Heritage site, and Jeff is effortlessly brilliant at his job. Every arch, apse, and arris holds an architectural secret he reveals with a playful story.

Stopping to inspect each menu, we learn that Austrian law requires authentic Wiener Schnitzel to be made with veal and served with a lemon slice, lingonberry jam, and parsley. In contrast, a mere pork schnitzel must be called *Wiener Schnitzel vom Schwein* or *Schnitzel Wiener Art.*

We learn that Wien is known as the City of Music, a creative melting-pot for Beethoven, Brahms, Bruckner, Haydn, Mahler, Mozart, Schoenberg, Schubert, and both Johann Strausses.

Jeff grabs us urgently by the arms in every narrow alleyway and pulls us into dark corners to share a local myth or fable.

—Listen, stop, look here — this is very, very important that you understand what I am about to tell you. Pay attention now...Look down, look down at your feet…

We look down.

We are standing on a metal grid over a deep hole, and a gnarly elf figure looks up at us. This is Lieber Augustin, a misfortunate troubadour from 1679 when the Great Plague struck Vienna. According to legend, Augustin had a little too much to drink, fell asleep in the street, and was dumped by the gravediggers into this hole, along with dozens of other plague victim bodies. The next day, when Augustin woke up with a hangover, he couldn't climb out, so he decided to play his pipes because he wanted to die the same way he lived. But his music was heard, and he was rescued, and miraculously didn't fall sick, despite having slept with the infected dead bodies. The Viennese attributed this miracle to his heavy drinking, and he has been a symbol of hope for all drinkers ever since.

This is clearly Jeff's favorite story, and it seems to make him thirsty, so he suggests we find a café to sit and drink beer. We've booked him for three hours, but he transcends conventional concepts like time and space. Like an Australian aboriginal crossing the outback along ancient songlines, Jeff navigates Vienna by his stories, not hours and minutes. We follow his Dreamtime tracks to navigate from palace to café to castle or cathedral and each watering hole.

—Jeff, how much would it cost to live in Vienna for a month? We ask over another pilsner.

He sucks deep on a Gauloise and squints as if quoting on a new water heater replacement. He explains that rents are artificially low and capped by inflation because, after the war, residents were grandfathered into rent deals, which could be passed on to children and other relatives. Many still pay a few hundred euros a month. He can find us something if we're interested.

Schooling is excellent and free, but you usually have to pay for *hort*, or afternoon school, where the kids stay and do fun activities till around 5.30 pm. This is expensive, he explains, about 200 euros a month.

Compared to America, it sounds like a budget fairytale land.

—Jeff, after hosting hundreds of tours, what's the most surprising thing you've learned about people from different countries?

He sucks deep again.

—I think it's that people like to talk about themselves a lot

He explains that even though visitors have traveled thousands of miles and booked him as a tour guide, they quickly get bored hearing about Vienna and insist on telling him about their city or their lives instead.

Sitting over a beer in the sun, this seems very true and meaningful, and we all reflect in silence. Yes, even we insist on talking about ourselves to Jeff.

—Oh là là! Cries Jeff again, looking over our shoulders at yet another beautiful woman.

This happens every ten minutes or so, like European performance art.

—Every Spring, I feel like this! Why are there so many beautiful women in Vienna?

It was presumably a rhetorical question, but we sympathize anyway. Jeff of Europe has been with us for seven hours, and we all need to rest. Besides, he was meant to be picking up his daughter a while back. He asks us for spare coins to buy another single cigarette from the table next door, so we give him a generous tip and hug him farewell.

There's one last thing I must address.

—One small suggestion, Jeff. Would you consider changing your professional name? Last night, I almost canceled when

I heard the name Jeff Thomas, because we thought you were American, not an authentic Austrian. Perhaps call yourself something German instead?

—Something German?

—You know. Wolfgang, Johann, or Helmut? Probably not Adolf, but you get the idea.

A crooked smile creeps across his lips.

—You know Jeff isn't my real name, right? he confides.

—Ah, well, it doesn't sound very French

—My real name is Jean-Michel; I hate it!

We all get the giggles again, and we hug once more, and with that, Jeff/Jean-Michel is gone forever.

Driving back the next day to Croatia, we reminisce about our day together. Without Jeff's goofy, eccentric lightness, something is missing. The Four Wieners are missing a Wiener.

We know our brush with Jeff represented something special, something rare and birdlike, something missing from our daily lives, an echo of our youth, but we can't put it into words.

It may just be Europe. Possibly, walking freely on a sunny day with good friends, Jeff of Europe reminds us that all this still exists. All over Europe, there are hundreds of beautiful, safe, affordable, walking towns and cities like this, with winding medieval alleys, cobblestones, cathedrals, and ancient stories to be revealed.

As much as we may love some of the privileges of living in America, or anywhere else, there is nowhere like Europe for making the heart sing. Its economic and military dominance are long gone, but its beauty will never fade.

So if you're ever wondering what you'll do with yourself

when you're old and retired, and you've saved a little money, and there's nowhere to be, then a thousand ancient piazzas across Europe will be waiting for you to wander, where you might enjoy an espresso, a pastry, and a good book in the morning sun.

Just make sure you find a Jeff to show you around.

HOW TO SURVIVE A NARCISSIST (ESPECIALLY IF IT'S YOU)

"Since the Universe has no center, you can't be it."
— Neil deGrasse Tyson

The first narcissist I had to navigate in the wild was an enormous, bald, Dutch pharmaceutical expatriate called Bart Bakker. It wasn't a fair match. He was enjoying the tail-end of his illustrious career, with a lucrative expat China President posting to Shanghai, sent out from the head office with deep experience to sell more drugs and generally terrorize the locals.

I was still in my early twenties, a barely-paid newspaper reporter from Hong Kong with zero business experience, trying to kickstart my marketing career with a Chinese advertising agency.

What could go wrong?

My first encounter with Bakker had gone poorly. He needed to launch a new laxative drug before his competitors, and our job was to conduct consumer research to recommend how to advertise it. The problem wasn't the research. Our intrepid research team had surveyed thousands of Chinese patients, and I came to the meeting armed with an encyclopedic knowledge of mainland bowel problems and constipation challenges.

I literally knew my shit.

The problem was my lack of meeting experience, and specifically my ignorance of that majestic beast, the Business Narcissist. I might have been better prepared if I'd started my career in the mail room, taken coffee orders for the team, and observed the grown-ups from the back of the conference room for a few years. Instead, I had been plucked prematurely from my journalist career and thrust into the hot seat, expected to present and defend my recommendations with big, bald Bart Bakker.

My first meeting in Shanghai with his team started badly.

— And so, as you can see from this first slide, I will share the results from our study and make our recommendation about these four concepts…

— Bakker has a question, he thundered.

— Pardon?

— Bakker wants to ask a question.

— What? Confused, I froze for too long.

Bakker had a question. Was there another Bakker in the room? Was the terrified Chinese lady sitting next to him Mrs. Bakker, perhaps? It was unpleasantly common for European expats to fall in love with and marry their assistants. Or, given his age, was one of the spotty, skinny-tied fellows the Son of Bakker?

No idea. Better stay quiet.

— Bakker's question is, why did we only test four concepts and not more? He demanded.

Ah, so he *was* Bakker, after all. Now, I just had to ignore this oddness and attempt an answer:

— We decided that having over four options for respondents

to compare would be excessive. We collaborated with your team to choose these concepts.

He was not happy with this. In the glare of the projector beam, I noticed steam wafting off his shiny head and saw that his team had their faces down, pretending to take meeting notes and avoiding eye contact.

— Bakker disapproves. Bakker says continue.

And so it continued, slide after slide for hours. Bakker disagrees. Bakker objects. Bakker cannot believe this number. Finally, and to everyone's relief, Bakker exits.

We agreed with his team to come back with a new presentation the following week, and we filed out in silence and headed back to our office. The research was good, and I knew I'd let my team down. When we reached our desks, my boss had already heard about the meeting and summoned me for a debrief. She was kind but disappointed, and I promised to nail it next time.

— You'd better, because I'll need to attend to make sure, she said, waving me out.

For days, I tried to make sense of the meeting. Where did I go wrong? Why would anyone refer to themselves in the third person? What does it tell you about their character, and how should you handle them? I started to develop a few theories. I decided that Bakker had spent too long as an expat in China, where nobody dared to challenge his authority, and he had become a Business Narcissist. He was an experiment in what happens when you take a middle-aged corporate Leviathan, separate him from his family and friends, and give him a kingdom to rule.

He was Kurtz in *Heart of Darkness*; Brando in *Apocalypse Now*.

The horror! The horror! I would need to find a way to deal with him on his terms.

The day of the second presentation arrived, and the stakes were raised. My boss would be watching, and my fledgling career was on the line. The lights went out, and I put the first slide on the screen.

— Last week, we were not prepared for Bakker. Bakker was unhappy. Bakker gave us wise advice based on his great knowledge of laxatives. Today, we have taken Bakker's suggestions, and we hope to please Bakker.

I stopped. It just sounded mad. I'd overdone the Bakkers. I caught my boss's eye, and she looked horrified. Even the minions had stopped pretending to take notes and looked up, horrified.

— Bakker APPROVES! he roared from the darkness with a single clap of his hands.

And we were off. The meeting was a success, and everyone was relieved, as were future generations of Chinese bowels. That day, I learned that sometimes, the best way to win over a man who has fallen in love with his reflection is to hold up a mirror for him to enjoy.

But, of course, that isn't always the best way to navigate the narcissists we meet. Sometimes, they are our parents, partners, or children (or even ourselves), and we must understand how to navigate them sensitively. In this essay, I'll explore the myth, the condition, the good and bad news, and end with an antidote.

Starting with the myth, it's worth taking a moment to enjoy the simple power of the Narcissus myth, which has survived for thousands of years. There are several different versions of the story, some focusing more on Echo, the girl who fatally fell in love with Narcissus. But I prefer the Greek version that keeps its focus on the danger of the unexamined male ego. Narcissus' mother was warned by the seer Teiresias that her son would live a long life as long as 'he never knows himself.' As her handsome lad grew up, he broke many hearts and caused great pain to women and men alike, but he never found love himself. Then, one day, he caught his reflection in a pool and fell in love with his reflection. Like that friend we all know who never met a mirror or shop window he didn't love, Narcissus could not leave his image in the pool and wasted away with unrequited love. His corpse rotted and became the beautiful flowers that today still bear his name.

First, the good news. We are unlikely to waste away with self-love. If we do feel special and suspect that we might be a narcissist, statistically, we are in good company, as Rutger Bregman notes:

> In the 1950s, only 12% of young adults agreed with the statement, "I'm a very special person." Today, 80% do, and the fact is, we're all becoming more and more alike. We all read the same bestsellers, watch the same blockbusters, and sport the same sneakers.

Narcissists do rather well for themselves. Elon Musk and Jeff Bezos became the wealthiest men on the planet. In politics, Donald Trump experimented with overt public narcissism and was elected to the White House with no political experience. In the mating game, it appears that narcissists are more interested in short-term relationships or hookups and, therefore, almost certainly more successful at passing on their 'selfish genes.' Perhaps narcissism serves an adaptive function, an increased success in short-term mating.

Many of us may be narcissists, but it's unlikely to be pathological. Narcissistic personality disorder, a dysfunction that might manifest as a lack of empathy, antagonism, grandiosity, and attention-seeking, only affects around one percent of the population, a level that has remained stable since clinicians started measuring it.

Finally, there's some relief for parents who might fear that by showering their kids with unconditional love, they might be raising future narcissists. It's a common assumption that the most self-centered adults must have received *too much* love as children. Mothers of sons especially get the blame for raising little princes. But in Alain de Botton's professional opinion, the reverse is more likely to be true:

> *We may think of egoists as people who have grown sick from too much love. But the opposite is the case: an egoist is someone who has not yet had their fill. Self-centredness has to have a clean run in the early years if it isn't to haunt and ruin the later ones. The so-called narcissist is simply a benighted soul who has not had a chance to be inordinately and unreasonably admired at the start.*

Now for the less good news: Our narcissistic blind spots often hold us back and cause suffering, both to others and ourselves, especially in relationships. When we love something about ourselves so profoundly that we always put it first, we cannot give our partners the love that they also need from us. It's as if we take their love, and instead of returning it or doubling it, we use it to feed our self-love.

At the start of a relationship, the things that make us unique and the way we love ourselves for it can become irresistible to our partners. They might lack and crave these traits themselves and, therefore, admire the natural confidence we have about them. However, self-love is never enough to feed a life together, and if we refuse to know ourselves and adapt, relationships harden into stubborn defensiveness and break down.

Ironically, the antidote to narcissism is not, as Teiresias warned, to 'never know yourself' but the opposite. The earlier we can identify our unique form of self-love, perhaps understand where it comes from, and accept it, the faster we can move on from it.

We must learn to gaze into the lake and see not just our reflection but also the lake and our self-love.

We need to see things as they are.

Our friends and family might guide us to know ourselves better, especially if we ask for their help. Often, it's the thing they've been teasing us about, which is a gift of deep love.

Feel free to pause here and give your self-love a name, even write it down. Go on; this essay can wait.

When we find it, we should first celebrate it because loving at least one thing about ourselves is far better than not loving ourselves at all. After celebrating it, we might be honest about how it holds us back and might have frustrated our partners, ended friendships, and cost us a job we had worked hard for.

Lastly, we must learn how to laugh about it. How would our bluntest school friend or sibling tease us about it? What would happen to us if we were a character in an episode of Seinfeld or The Simpsons? If we genuinely think we're always the most intelligent person in the room, then that's funny. If we check out our left side profile in every mirror, but never our right side, that is also promising comedy material.

They say the wise take the business of laughing at themselves very seriously.

But neither Narcissus, nor Bakker, were ever in on the joke.

1990: THE FORGOTTEN YEAR OF FREEDOM

When I turned 17, my world narrowed sharply. I caught a mystery virus that knocked me out, and I spent over a year in bed, barely able to walk or keep my eyes open for more than an hour. My parents took me to see all kinds of doctors, but none could diagnose whether it was physical or psychological. Whatever the cause, after a year in bed, I was depressed. I remember little about that period other than recurring thoughts of suicide and the terror of never recovering.

But when I turned 18, my illness, my future, and the world's political fault lines all changed almost overnight, resulting in a long and unexpected adventure across the Middle East and Eastern Europe.

The Berlin Wall came down in November 1989, and a few weeks later, on my 18th birthday, December 3rd, Soviet leader Mikhail Gorbachev and President George H. W. Bush declared that a new, permanent era of peace had begun. Peace? I'd been an adult for precisely one day, and the Cold War of my entire childhood was over!

Freedom swept across Europe. The Romanians overthrew the Communist government, executing Nicolae Ceaușescu and his wife. A week later, the playwright Václav Havel became president of the now-free Czechoslovakia. Throughout 1990, millions of Europeans got their first taste of freedom, and many more countries declared independence from the Soviet Union—Poland, Lithuania, Bulgaria, Estonia, and Armenia. Gorbachev resigned with perfect ironic timing on Christmas Day, 1991, and they lowered the hammer and sickle over the Kremlin for the last time.

1990 was also to become my year of freedom.

The same week as my 18th birthday, I received a letter with an 'Unconditional Offer' to study at Oxford University. I'd passed the exam and interview, which meant I only required 2 A-levels at grade E or above. It was a miracle. I understand they no longer make those offers, but it changed the trajectory of my life.

My health soon started to improve, presumably because the pressure of falling behind was gone. All thoughts of suicide ended and have thankfully never returned.

My heart breaks now when I hear that a friend or a teenager is struggling with depression: it's a club with a lifetime membership.

I no longer needed to attend school, so I dropped out, flew to Israel, where I lived and worked for several months, and then started island-hopping and hitchhiking across Greece and Turkey and back toward Eastern Europe. It was almost a year before I reached home; I had no plan or money. I was eighteen years old and wanted to meet girls, enjoy my new freedom, and be part of the historical euphoria in Eastern Europe. But it was mainly about the girls!

I was truly alone and free, as was still possible then. I had no credit card, email, or mobile phone and never more than a few dollars in my pocket. It would be a dozen years before the word 'Selfie' would be coined for the first time, and it never once occurred to me to photograph my food before eating it. My parents only received a few postcards from random locations and must have been worried the whole year. It was bliss — total teenage independence — which sadly no longer exists.

I hitchhiked everywhere, slept on sofas and beaches, washed dishes in kitchens for meals, rented out snorkels, shaved heads, and made appalling fluorescent jewelry, which I sold sitting on a black cloth outside Greek island nightclubs. It was a big revelation to learn that if you kept moving and hustling, like a rolling stone, you could keep going as long as you wanted to. Life becomes very simple when you only need to make enough money to eat, sleep, and hitch to the next town. It would terrify me now, but I don't remember ever experiencing fear back then.

Finally, my luck ran out in Istanbul. I'd made my way across Turkey from the ancient stone heads of Nemrut Dağı in the east to the troglodyte caves of Cappadocia and the ruins of Troy and Aphrodisia. I had been working the streets around the Blue Mosque for a few weeks, hustling to bring backpackers to where I earned a commission — a leather shop, a carpet seller, a hotel, a restaurant, and a travel agent.

One day, I realized that if I also wandered all day wearing my backpack, it became easier to win the trust of other tourists arriving off the buses! Soon, I was earning decent commissions and was close to saving enough money to cross Eastern Europe on my way home. But my hustling had not gone unnoticed by all the Turkish street kids in leather jackets working the same district as me, and one evening, they surrounded me in an alley, pushed me against a wall, and flashed a knife blade.

We all agreed it was time for me to move on, and I thanked them for their kind suggestion.

The other travelers in my hostel who had just arrived from Prague and Berlin told magical stories about the Independence celebrations across Eastern Europe. I was desperate to be part of the unfolding history. I hadn't saved as much as I'd planned, but early the following day, I caught a bus to the Bulgarian border and hitch-hiked from there to Sofia, hoping I wasn't too late for the party.

I wasn't. The irrepressible joy of freedom was still alive everywhere, and it changed me forever. In 1990, on the streets of Eastern Europe, everything seemed possible again. In Sofia, Budapest, Berlin, and Prague, everyone was out in the streets and wanted to talk all night, even to a penniless kid like me. Everyone had a sofa to sleep on, a crate of pilsner, and a big idea for their lives and country. They would argue about politics for hours, and now and again, they would remember I was in the room and translated a summary into English.

I would nod to show I understood, but I didn't. As they argued, I started to feel grateful for the freedom I had always taken for granted.

It reminded me of the nights I slept around the fires on the beaches in Eilat with all the Israeli soldiers, boys and girls barely older than me, who were on leave, fresh from the intensity of the Occupied Territories. They were trying to steal a few days of teenage beach life while still clutching the machine guns that could not leave their sight. They were sad and confused, and their guitar songs and conversations were about fighting for a simpler and more peaceful future. As soon as they could quit the army, they plotted to escape Israel to bum around India and Southeast Asia, where their dollars might afford them a year or more of freedom.

Everyone, it seemed, just wanted to be free.

I remember one night in Prague when a room full of college students lost all patience trying to make me understand what it meant to live in a police state. They explained how they hadn't known who to trust, even their school friends. I wanted to laugh and say, "I know that feeling," but I really didn't. They planned to visit London or New York as soon as possible and to move there one day. The Velvet Revolution had changed everything for them and the aperture of their hopes for the future. They could see in my eyes that I didn't understand. I had only experienced freedom my whole life, and I took it for granted. With my British passport, I could roam freely across borders.

Hardly anyone outside Eastern Europe talks about 1990 anymore, especially in America, where I live. That worries me. If we collectively forget what it means for people to break free, we might fail to support our democratic partners when they need us. When I watch the news and see how fiercely the Ukrainians are willing to fight to remain free, I recall being young and ignorant in 1990, and I know who we need to support now and why.

I didn't understand it then, but it was a great privilege to be 18 in 1990.

First, it was the year I learned that being healthy is the most important freedom of all.

Then I discovered that you don't need much money when you're young to roam free and happy across most of the world.

Lastly, on the streets of Eastern Europe, I learned that nothing is more important for a society than protecting its hard-won freedoms.

COOKING FOR
FORTY SILENT STRANGERS

This summer, I tried something different. From Utah, I drove with my twenty-year-old son and his girlfriend over the mountains to Lava Hot Springs, Idaho, where I would work from 5 am to 9 pm for ten days, cooking and cleaning for forty silent strangers.

My son and I had attended a ten-day silent Vipassana meditation retreat together before, but this was my first time volunteering as a server. After arriving at the center, I handed over my mobile phone and valuables, cleared the bugs off the foam bed in my outhouse, and set to work washing dishes. For the next ten days, I worked quietly with my four fellow servers from 5 am onwards to ensure that our forty silent sitters, including my son and his girlfriend, were well-nourished as they struggled through long days of self-imposed silent meditation.

Between peeling endless pounds of vegetables, preparing and serving (surprisingly complex) menus, and clearing, handwashing, and sanitizing everything in sight, we clambered up the hill to join three meditation sessions each day in the main hall. We ended each day with a final evening server group meeting, during which I struggled and often failed to stay awake.

The obvious question is: *Why would I ever sign up for this?*

I'll try my best to answer this, and while I'm at it, a few other questions: *What was surprising? Did I learn anything? And would I do it again?*

First, I should describe a Vipassana meditation retreat. You might skip this part if you're already familiar with the tradition. You can also learn about it at dhamma.org, where anyone can reserve a free place on a course at over 300 locations worldwide.

Vipassana, which means *to see things as they really are*, is one of the oldest and simplest meditation techniques. Buddha rediscovered it over 2500 years ago and taught it as a universal remedy for human suffering. Once very prevalent in India, it died out and was almost lost forever, but it survived amongst Buddhist monks in Myanmar and was reintroduced to India in the 1970s. It has spread globally ever since.

The technique is non-religious and free to learn, and participants donate whatever they want to at the end of each course. The standard silent course is a challenging eleven days long, although shorter and longer versions are available. Participants are encouraged to maintain a daily practice in between retreats.

Yuval Noah Harari, the Israeli historian and brilliant author of 'Sapiens', once described discovering Vipassana in his early twenties:

"The most important thing I realized was that the deep source of my suffering is in the patterns of my own mind. When I want something and it doesn't happen, my mind reacts by generating suffering. Suffering is not an objective condition in the outside world. It is a mental reaction generated by my own mind."

I also wrote about it in the chapter 'Her Story' in my novel *Path*, when the girl describes her retreat to the boy:

"We were just sitting in silence, paying attention to our breath, the air coming out of our nostrils, the sensation on our upper lip. It was all very simple, practical, and not religious at all. It immediately started to have a profound effect on me.

From that first hour, I learned that I had almost no control over my mind, and my attention would spring like a grasshopper between past memories and anxiety about the future. Despite all my attempts to stay 'in the now.' The harder I tried, the worse it was. It was like somebody else was endlessly channel-flicking on a TV set I was trying to watch.

They told us to focus on our normal breath through the nose, to keep going, to stick to our practice with persistence. But after several hours, my brain ached. It was brutal. The hardest thing I've ever tried to do. After a few days, I slowly got the hang of it and learned to meditate using the rising and fading sensations in my body. I could observe my thoughts, but I still suffered setbacks and frustrations."

So why did I volunteer as a server this time instead of joining again as a sitter? First, it was my turn. Other volunteers had served me at my previous retreats, so it was my turn to help others learn this valuable technique from which I had benefited.

Second, I was curious to understand more about how things work 'behind the scenes' at a retreat center, but more importantly, how to unlock the full power of mettā, a form of compassion usually translated as loving-kindness. I had often read and heard Buddhist teachers talking about the enormous positive energy that can be generated through a form of meditation called mettā-bhāvanā, but I had still not experienced it consistently myself. I was curious. What if I could learn to harness this positive energy for myself and others through serving and meditation?

Third, like any parent, I felt responsible for the emotional health of my son and his girlfriend, who was still only 18 at the time. I had introduced them to Vipassana, and although I trusted the process, I still had fears, given their ages. I didn't want to interfere with their spiritual journey, but I wanted to watch over them and intervene if necessary. So much for letting go! I'm a hypocrite: I love making fun of 'helicopter parents,' but I'm hardly any better!

In short, I signed up out of duty, curiosity, and parental anxiety.

What was the serving experience like versus my expectations? It was far more physically challenging than I had expected. A Vipassana retreat day starts with a gong at 4 am, finishes around 9 pm, and follows a punctual itinerary. For instance, in the kitchen, we had to make sure breakfast for forty was laid out and served by 6.30 am, including cooked oatmeal, toast, cereals, fruit, and every imaginable variety of tea, milk, and condiments. Then everything needed to be cleared or refrigerated, wiped down and hand washed and sanitized by 7.52 am, giving us 8 minutes to sprint a quarter mile up the hill to join the 8 am sitting. An hour later, we had to race back down to continue preparing and serving the complex vegetarian recipes each day by 11 am. Then clear, wash, sanitize, peel, and repeat for ten days.

To make things even tougher, I had decided to follow the fasting schedule for 'Old' (returning) students, which meant I fasted between 11 a.m. and breakfast the next day. After the first two days, I reframed it as a much-needed fitness boot camp once I realized how physically demanding the routine was. Sure enough, I lost a dozen pounds by the end.

While the experience was more physically demanding than expected, it was less mentally challenging than being a sitter. We typically only had time to sit silently for three hour-long sessions each day, so there was less scope for introspection. Instead of sharing a room with a silent stranger, I had a basic room to myself, which also helped. Also in the kitchen we were allowed to talk and get to know each other. Servers should limit conversation to task-related issues, but we got to know each other well over the ten days.

The camaraderie that slowly developed between our small group was intense and unexpected, and we continued to stay in touch afterward. Perhaps we were blessed to be part of a uniquely kind, authentic, and joyful band of souls from all walks of life, or else it's just a natural outcome when any small team works intensely on a common, altruistic purpose. I have no way to prove this, but I suspect the rare purity of our intent together for a common goal — to serve the forty silent, struggling sitters — was why the bonds were so strong. Either way, I had not expected to find such a joyful sense of community on a silent meditation course.

Another surprise was how difficult I found it to meditate

while serving. As a sitter, I can get into a strong rhythm on a retreat, and by day three or so, my 'monkey mind' has calmed down. I can consistently observe my thoughts come and go and experience the energy flowing around my body. My daily practice at home also usually goes well. But as a server, I found it almost impossible to stop thinking about peeling vegetables and washing dishes. With all the physical exertion and the kitchen conversation, I struggled to switch between action mode and calm mode, and at times, it was frustrating. I suspect and hope that things will go better a second time now that I've learned the ropes and processed the server role.

To sum up, the whole experience was more physical, more joyful, less emotionally challenging, and less calming than I expected.

However, it was still deeply spiritual in one crucial way: loving-kindness.

When I look back on what I learned through serving, and what has stayed with me in my daily life (apart from a dozen tasty new recipes!) I think of mettā-bhāvanā, the loving-kindness meditation that we practiced together every night. I knew mettā was an important aspect of Vipassana, but until I decided to serve myself and then practice it each evening together with our group, I hadn't appreciated its full benefit.

On the face of it, the mettā meditation appears like a religious prayer, or a gratitude diary entry, as in lines like these:

May all beings be happy; May they all be secure.

May they all see good fortune; May no evil befall them.

May no suffering befall them; May no sorrow befall them.

And like a Christian prayer, there's space to include specific people or groups that are in our thoughts for whatever reason. In my experience during a retreat there's always a 'pareto' effect, where one person in my life occupies 80% of my mental energy all week. Perhaps they are struggling, or we are fighting, and no matter how much I want to move on, I keep returning to think about them. Mettā allows me to direct my love and energy to this person. However, it's something different and deeper than a petition to a powerful god:

Mettā is not prayer; nor is it the hope that an outside agency will help. On the contrary, it is a dynamic process, producing a supportive atmosphere where others can act to help themselves. Mettā can be omni-directional or directed toward a particular person. In either case, meditators are simply providing an outlet; because the mettā we feel is not 'our' mettā. By eliminating egotism, we open our minds and make them conduits for the forces of positivity throughout the universe.

—Vipassana research Institute

Mettā is not something that can be directly 'understood' intellectually, it has to be practiced *after* Vipassana, to transport us beyond our aversions and clinging thoughts:

So long as negativities such as aversion dominate the mind, it is futile to formulate conscious thoughts of goodwill, and doing so would be a ritual devoid of inner meaning. However, when negativities are removed by the practice of Vipassana, goodwill naturally wells up in the mind; and emerging from the prison of self-obsession, we begin to concern ourselves with the welfare of others.

For me, the big learning was that Vipassana and Mettā are like two wings of a bird. They only make sense together. Without Mettā, the practice of Vipassana soon becomes egocentric. Without Vipassana, our minds are not calm and pure enough to generate Mettā for others:

> *Mettā works only when it is the spontaneous overflow of a purified mind…What, after all, is the purpose of freeing ourselves of negativity and egotism unless we share these benefits with others? In a retreat, we cut ourselves off from the world temporarily in order to return and share with others what we have gained in solitude. These two aspects of the practice of Vipassana are inseparable.*

I suspect this must be experienced personally rather than explained. Still, I want to share one last passage, this time from the British-born Tibetan nun Jetsunma Tenzin Palmo, who lived alone in a cave in India for 11 years:

> *Compassion is extraordinarily important in the spiritual path. It's the other side of the coin: we have both wisdom and compassion. The greater the understanding of the inherent pain in beings—the more the mind becomes very clear, as if wiping away dust from the eyes—the more one sees the underlying pain in people's lives, and the more compassion arises. Even if overtly people don't look like they are suffering, we see that under the façade there is a lot of pain and many problems.*
>
> *Naturally, then compassion arises, and the two feed each other. Compassion without wisdom is sterile; it is blind. It's like having legs but no eyes. Wisdom without compassion is like being crippled; you can't go anywhere. So, we need the two, and*

they mutually support each other because it's not just that the intellect has to be open, the heart also has to be open. They are indivisible. Wisdom and compassion are like two wings. We cannot fly with one alone.

—Into the Heart of Life, Jetsunma Tenzin Palmo

As for the final question, would I choose to serve again? Yes, I would. I enjoy and believe in it. I know Vipassana helps people calm their minds because it's worked for me and others. It's an idea worth spreading, and when I serve, I can watch it spreading.

Before this summer, I understood how to practice Vipassana. After cooking for forty strangers, I also understand why.

LUNA LUNA: THE GREATEST
ART STORY EVER TOLD

I spent Saturday afternoon exploring a 60,000-square-foot L.A. warehouse trying to make sense of Luna Luna, perhaps the greatest art story ever told.

It spans six decades and features Jean-Michel Basquiat, Roy Lichtenstein, Salvador Dalí, David Hockney, Keith Haring, Kenny Scharf, Miles Davis, Philip Glass, and a $100m investment led by the Canadian rapper Drake. The tale begins in cold-war Vienna and Hamburg against a backdrop of post-war Holocaust trauma. If it were a painting, it would feature dark, European surrealist roots, neon-colored graffiti of New York's pop-art explosion, and a long sandy exile in the Texas desert in 44 metal container boxes.

It reminds us that art does not need to be confined to individual frames on well-lit gallery walls in capital cities, or the vaults of billionaires. Art also lives. Outside the constraints of the boxes created by their industry, artists can collaborate and create physical spaces for crowds to enjoy together for reasons other than money. It leaves us wanting more.

Luna Luna is a forgotten fantasy and perhaps the greatest story that art has ever told. I will explore it here in three action-filled acts.

ACT I, HAMBURG 1987: *THE MOST DIZZYING, DAZZLING ART SHOW ON EARTH*

Over a seven-week run in Hamburg in the summer of 1987, almost 300,000 visitors came to enjoy a colorful, surreal amusement park built by the eccentric Austrian maverick André Heller and 32 of the world's most talented artists. Delighted German families rode in a large, white Ferris wheel designed by Jean-Michel Basquiat, rotating to Miles Davis's haunting track 'Tutu.' They explored the mirrored Dalídom of Salvador Dalí and wandered through Roy Lichtenstein's glass maze, to a soundtrack composed by Philip Glass. They could step inside David Hockney's 'Enchanted Tree' structure or whizz around on Keith Haring's painted carousel or Kenny Scharf's chair swing ride.

It was a big hit, fusing pop art and surrealism with abstraction, art brut, Dada, nouveau realism, and Viennese Actionism. Life magazine called it the most dizzying, dazzling art show on Earth. Heller united established post-war artists like Dali, Hockney, and Lichtenstein, with emerging stars like Haring, Basquiat, and Scharf. Even Andy Warhol, who didn't take part and died a few months before the show, was memorialized in a booth where visitors could get their 15-minutes-of-fame snaps with cut-outs of Einstein and Marilyn Monroe.

It was joyful. From a 30-minute documentary video shown on Saturday, we sense the true magic of the 1987 live carnival. Kids squeal with delight and roam wild, as couples cuddle and enjoy a mock wedding at Heller's surreal wedding chapel, surrounded by jugglers, magicians, stilt-walkers, and costumed performers.

To remind us that this is 1980's Europe (and not prudish 2024 California) a screen shows the sniggering audience of Manfred Deix's *Palace of the Winds*, a live performance of amplified bare-cheeked farting, accompanied by a concert violinist, an homage to the public 'flatulists' in Europe earlier in the century.

And then it ended. After one summer of fun, Luna Luna was packed up into containers, ready to be shipped to the next destination. As they meticulously labeled everything for a future event, nobody dreamed it would be forgotten for almost forty years.

But who was Heller, how did he come up with such a colossal idea, and how did he pull it off? Franz André Heller was born in 1947 in Vienna into a wealthy Jewish family of sweets manufacturers, Gustav and Wilhelm Heller. In 1964, he began a prolific and eclectic creative career as a German-language artist, author, poet, singer, songwriter, and actor. Sixty years on, he's still going.

The idea for Luna Luna was inspired by his childhood memories of the *Prater* amusement park in Vienna, and a strong desire to bring progressive, avant-garde art into the lives of people who seldom visit galleries and museums. In short, he wanted to bring great artists together, and then share their art with the masses.

But it took him a decade to pull it off. His first meeting was in Paris in 1976 with Sonia Delaunay, the Ukrainian-born artist who co-founded the Simultané movement and designed the Luna Luna entrance archway, finished posthumously in 1979.

Heller persisted with his vision. After turning down funding from McDonald's, in 1985 he closed a grant for $350,000 from a German magazine and started traveling to visit the world's most talented artists. With a budget of only $10,000 each, he had to inspire them into acceptance. In his own words, this was the pitch:

"Listen, you are constantly getting the greatest commissions. Everyone wants your paintings or sculptures, but I am inviting you to take a trip back to your own childhood. You can design your very own amusement park, just as you think would be right today, and really, without exception, everyone answered by saying, sure, that's a nice, pleasant challenge."

Eventually, the ball got rolling and the artists themselves started making introductions. Warhol sent Heller to meet Basquiat, Lichtenstein introduced Hockney, and Haring brought him to see Kenny Scharf.

Haring and Scharf relocated to Austria to build their attractions by hand, and the scale of their output is remarkable: apart from the carousel, I counted eight enormous bus-sized original Haring banners. The documentary shows Kenny Scharf building six large goofy sculptures and hand-painting over 100 colorful panels for his chair swing.

However, most of the American artists worked remotely with Heller's team, who provided the resources they needed. For instance, Basquiat's Ferris wheel and the Dalídom were built by Viennese opera and theater workers from vintage carnival attractions. It was the only time Basquiat ever allowed one of his works to be painted remotely, and the 1933 white wooden wheel is covered with dozens of his slogans and sketches, topped with a giant monkey's butt at the rear! Basquiat's sisters have since shared that their brother loved visiting Coney Island as a kid and would have approved.

I wasn't aware of how old the original attractions were, and I couldn't understand why the attendant warned me they were 'probably over a hundred years old' when I stepped into Lichtenstein's glass and mirror maze. I had never walked into a piece of pop art before, and it gave me goosebumps to know that it had a pre-war history all of its own.

ACT II, TEXAS: FORTY YEARS IN THE DESERT

After such a successful debut in Hamburg, Heller believed he had options. It looked like Vienna's city council would buy the park for permanent display, but this fell through. It was rumored to be heading to the Netherlands at one point, and a US tour was also explored. A wider European tour also went nowhere, and the storage fees mounted up, sending Heller into debt.

He ran out of runway. Finally, he agreed to sell Luna Luna for around $6 million to a Delaware-based philanthropic group, the Stephen and Mary Birch Foundation. They intended to recreate it in San Diego's Balboa Park and an LA Times article in 1991 suggested it was a done deal: "What seemed impossible has become all but definite: A local arts venture has won the enthusiastic support of both arts professionals and city officials."

But again, the relaunch fell through because of a dispute about charging commission and various rights concerns, and the ownership went into decades of litigation. As the legal issues dragged on, the 44 containers were shipped to rural Texas, where they sat baking by the side of a road, accompanied by rattlesnakes, armadillos, and scorpions.

Meanwhile, the art world moved on and forgot all about Luna Luna. Perhaps because it took place in Germany and before the internet and smartphones, it didn't take long for the memories to disappear. For instance, I personally stayed in a commune in Hamburg in 1990, and nobody mentioned its name.

Why was Luna Luna forgotten? Of course, great art often goes missing and must be rediscovered, but this was on such a uniquely public scale that our collective amnesia seems odd. Perhaps because it sought to disrupt the art industry's control of value and meaning through its arteries of auctions, museums, and galleries? Was Heller's ambition a threat to the establishment: to bring the artists together and then art to the masses?

Others tried to replicate it. In 2015, Banksy, another artist operating outside the establishment, created a darker sort of bizarro Luna Luna "bemusement park" called Dismaland in England. Banksy persuaded 58 artists, including Jenny Holzer, Damien Hirst, Jeff Gillette, and Jimmy Cauty, to contribute, and described it as a "family theme park unsuitable for children." Over a five-week run, it attracted a respectable 150,000 visitors, but they couldn't interact with the art, and it left the critics cold.

Arguably, Weston-super-Mare, the seaside town he chose for his dystopian vision, already does a respectable job at evoking the apocalypse even without the input of 58 visiting artists.

During these years, there were plenty of wealthy suitors for Luna Luna, but none would commit without an inspection. The sellers insisted that the 44 containers be purchased as-is, sight unseen, which put buyers off. One potential buyer was permitted a limited inspection in 2018 and opened the door to find water sloshing around.

In 2018, a niche art and design review website, Minnie Muse, profiled Luna Luna artfully with photographs. This caught the attention of Michael Goldberg, a creative director in the US. Goldberg saw the potential for resurrection and brought the idea to Drake's DreamCrew. Everyone instantly fell in love with the idea, and things moved quickly with Heller. A deal was made. Nobody knows precisely how much they paid or how it was structured, but it's rumored that the overall investment in relaunching the carnival is over $100 million—the price, say, of a single Picasso or Klimt in 2023.

One extra kink in the story involves Heller himself. In 2017 the eccentric Austrian became involved with the sale of an unusual Basquiat piece, which went on offer for $3 million. According to Austrian news magazine Falter, Heller glued sketches by Basquiat to strips of wood, applied red paint, and hammered nails and pieces of a black broom handle. Then a genuine portrait by Basquiat, acquired by Heller in 1990, was placed in the frame.

"In retrospect, the whole thing is, firstly, a childish prank. Secondly, it is naturally showing off. And thirdly, it is a stupid mixture of fiction and truth…Just a private fairy tale," Heller told Falter.

He could almost have been describing Luna Luna itself, in all the best ways! Heller has refuted any allegations of forgery and has since bought the frame back, but the incident damaged his credibility, and he is no longer involved with the project he gave birth to. He continues to cheer from the sidelines, though, and appears ecstatic about its revival.

ACT III, LOS ANGELES: EXCAVATION & RESURRECTION

In January 2022, the carnival left Texas for its new home, Los Angeles, in 44 containers, two wagons, and seven crates. It was time for the hard work of excavation and a set of tough decisions to ensure a successful resurrection.

In many ways, Southern California is the ideal next destination. First, La La Land is where the biggest and boldest stories are told and distributed worldwide. Second, ever since Disney opened the first modern amusement park in Anaheim in 1955, it has also become the spiritual home of the carnival. Third, those containers were originally shipped to San Diego back in 1990, and now they have (almost) reached their destination.

Drake's DreamCrew management team and Live Nation were a great fit for the next chapter. If you can handle the technical and artistic production challenges of a multi-city concert tour, presumably reconstructing a carnival feels manageable. And it likely also helped that back in 1987, each attraction was fastidiously packed and labeled by Germans and Austrians!

Drake was invested in getting it right: "It's such a unique and special way to experience art. This is a big idea and opportunity that centers around what we love most: bringing people together."

Another lucky break was the archive of Sabina Sarnitz, the Austrian underground photographer who captured Luna Luna's development in over ten thousand photographs across multiple cities in 1986-7. With her Nikon and Sinar cameras, she often used long exposures and supplemental spotlights to profile the crowds at the fairgrounds and the work of artists, technicians, artisans, architects, and studio teams. Sarnitz captured everything. Together with a detailed event book published by Heller, the photos not only helped the crew reconstruct the attractions, but they also now feature as fascinating mood boards as part of the new exhibition itself.

The new owners set about opening the containers, rebuilding the attractions in a 60,000-square-foot Boyle Heights warehouse, and sprinted fast to reopen the carnival. They launched in December 2023, just in time for Christmas, and opened to positive reviews and busy crowds. The tickets cost $38 on weekdays and $48 on weekends, and there's also a $85 VIP "Moon Pass," which gives visitors the opportunity to interact with various attractions.

The carousels and Ferris wheels of Luna Luna are turning again, at least until 'Spring '24' at this location. But did they get it right? With all the trade-offs between 'art' and 'amusement,' cost and safety, physical works, and multimedia storytelling, have they been faithful to the original intentions? And after almost forty years in the metaphorical and literal desert, what does it all mean?

I think they pulled it off. It was the most memorable art experience of my life, even inching past a glorious Hockney immersive 2023 retrospective in London. There were so many ways they could have gone off-piste, but they told this remarkable story, with a perfect balance of colorful joy and challenging ideas.

Here are just a few of my highlight experiences:

— Stepping into the first enormous room and being hit

by the vibrant neon colors of the revolving Kenny Scharf chair swing and the Keith Haring carousel

— Squirming at the videos of bare butt-cheeks farting a waltz outside the graphically painted facade of Manfred Deix's 'Palace of the Winds'.

— Discovering the full industrial scale of the eight bus-sized joyful Haring tarps, each hand-painted

— Navigating Lichtenstein's Luna Luna Pavilion hundred-year-old glass/mirror maze

— Following the curated timeline wall installation, which weaves European history with major art movements and the artists' own lives

— Lying on bean bags watching a 30-minute documentary (Favorite moment: when David Hockney sees what other artists are doing and admits that his installation might be a 'bit boring' in comparison)

— Seeing inside two example containers, half-full of carnival treasures, including a 'meta' film showing the original unboxing moment

— Taking part in a costumed mock wedding ceremony in Heller's cosmic chapel, complete with a live audience, polaroid still photo, and marriage certificate

— The gift shop sells original 'archival' items from the containers, including large posters (starting $225) and 40-year-old T-shirts (starting $250). I hate gift shops, but even I was tempted to own a piece of this history.

How could it be an even better experience? Perhaps they might dial up the live fairground entertainers, to recreate the vibe of the original event. Or they could make one of the moving attractions available to ride, for the same reason. But why? This is now art, not an amusement park. It's art because of its story and the collective cultural importance of its creators.

We don't need to sit on art to enjoy and learn from it.

It would have been less meaningful if Luna Luna had been simply playful. There are darker and more challenging moments, more faithful to the reality of a divided, cold-war Germany in 1987, still a few years before the Berlin Wall came down. Many of the artists were Jewish, including Heller, and if you scratch the surface of the more avant-garde European art movements, you feel the brutality of a haunting recent past might be revealed. We see it in Daniel Spoerri's Crap Chancellery, a spoof replica of Albert Speer's designs for Adolf Hitler's Reich Chancellery, an architectural symbol of Nazi grandeur and power. Nazis murdered Spoerri's father in World War II. The columns are topped with piles of excrement, and the interior of the original doubled as both an actual bathroom and a gallery of grotesque sculpture.

Perhaps most dark, the documentary features the *Mechanical Theater of robots and mannequins* built by British-Swiss artist Jim Whiting. Constructed from found objects and discarded junk, the torso-less dancing trousers and thrusting human-machine figures — at a bar or suspended above a car crash — create ghoulish scenes of alienation. The mannequins (thank God!) are no longer connected to their electronic motors and now sit lifeless and menacing. One is labeled 'Man watching porno.' I don't know the plan for them, and I'm in no hurry for them to resurrect this attraction.

EPILOGUE: THE GREATEST STORY

We may believe we go out to appreciate art because we find it beautiful, inspirational, or awe-inspiring. But the market often suggests otherwise. The value of art increases in proportion to the power of its story. The lives of da Vinci, Picasso, Van Gogh, Gauguin, and Basquiat all tell a memorable tale.

We need a narrative to connect with art meaningfully.

Story is meaning.

Does Luna Luna tell a compelling story? In the marketplace of ideas, is it strong enough to stand the test of time and outlast our tendency to move on and forget? After all, it's happened once already.

I believe it does, and even more so now because those forty years in the desert have strengthened it. It was a compelling story in 1987, but each talented artist was still emerging then. While those 44 containers baked in the Texas sun, each became more iconic and famous as an individual. Together, they are irresistible.

And now, after a few false starts, Luna Luna has experienced the most powerful story we know: the arc of struggle, death, entombment, and glorious resurrection.

The door to the tomb has been rolled away. The story might last two thousand years.

GOOD NEWS! NOBODY REALLY CARES ABOUT YOU

"I learned that the best way to take all people, black or white, is to take them for what they think they are, then leave them alone."
— William Faulkner

One early business trip to New York, a waitress at an uber-fancy restaurant effortlessly shamed me. It was the night before our IPO-listing, and our 'wunch' of Goldman Sachs investment bankers were competing to order the finest wines we'd ever tasted. This wasn't hard.

Ultimately, we were paying for it, but it still felt like we were being treated.

— More wine? She asked down her nose, unsmiling, extending a pale, willowy arm towards my half-filled glass.

— I'm sorry, I said, placing my hand on top of the glass. It's a different bottle.

— What? She hissed, painted eyebrows all angry.

— Sorry, I repeated, smiling nervously. I just mean, this wine's from a different bottle than that one. I didn't want to mix the wines.

— What?

I knew almost nothing about wine, but even I knew this.

The table fell silent. The eyebrows were furious now. I

grasped to help her save face.

— Oh, don't worry, fill her up! I was only trying to look sophisticated! I joked

— Leave sophistication to me

And with that, she glided away. Welcome to the Big Apple.

It was a great line. Everyone at our table whooped, enjoyed my embarrassment for a few minutes, and then completely erased it from their memories. Twenty-five years later, I can still recall every word, but mostly how it felt to judge and be judged.

It's simple, right? The less we evaluate others, and care about being evaluated, the lighter we will become. But even as I write this, I pause to consider my spelling choices. *Judgment?* Or *Judgement* with an 'e'? The first version is from America, where I live today. The second is British, where I was born, and is also correct in Singapore, where I lived for over a decade. Many of my readers will find the American spelling jarring and might believe I got it wrong or, worse, have adopted a new style to attract more American readers. Even my family in England might agree. But if I revert to the British spelling, the Americans will find it odd or old-fashioned. When both sets of readers will judge my spelling differently, which should I choose? Perhaps I could alternate, but that would seem sloppy.

Anyway, back to avoiding judgment: not so simple!

Let's start with a question: *Can we learn to stop judging others?* Yes, it's possible, but only if we first accept that we ourselves are far less 'fixed' and knowable than we believe. For example, when we try to sit silently with our thoughts for a few minutes, we can't go sixty seconds without losing control of them.

Stop reading and try it.

Our minds jump between past regrets and future worries, always rising and falling, with nobody at the steering wheel. We might also note how much we change during a lifetime. We have all grown up, or at least sideways, a great deal since childhood, and we're not the same person you would have met last year, or a month ago, or possibly even this morning. We are fluid and dynamic, and we expect to keep evolving in the future, so how could we be perfect today?

It can be a liberating idea: If we see ourselves as adaptable and improving, we might judge others less frequently.

And besides, there are no strengths without weaknesses, and no single person possesses all virtues. We know hundreds if not thousands of people, and we expect each of them to perform a specific 'role' in our lives. They likely require just one virtue to play that role well, so why would we expect them to possess every virtue?

Why judge others for falling short when we might equally have empathy for them? We all carry wounds and scars. Amchok Rinpoche once said that if we could see the true nature of living beings, we would have nothing but love and compassion for them. Or as the French philosopher Alain wrote:

Never say that people are evil…You just need to look for the pin.

The pin is a helpful image. When someone is angry with us and raises their voice, rather than becoming defensive or worse, we might imagine the source of their pain, their pin, and have compassion. Not judging others is one of the greatest gifts we can offer them. In the presence of someone who doesn't judge us, we find an open space to be ourselves; we are comforted and liberated.

A second question is also intriguing: *How might we ignore the critical scrutiny of others?* And even if we could avoid judgment, wouldn't we miss all that valuable feedback?

The truth is, nobody judges you. Nobody really cares about you.

Everyone is so busy worrying about themselves that they have very little time to judge you. You might *feel* their gaze and sense your ears burning up, or hear third-hand what someone thinks about you, but you can safely assume nobody thinks about you for more than thirty seconds a day. Perhaps more accurately, they might *care for you* but are too busy coping with life to stop and judge you. Paradoxically, we might find this news brutal and disturbing, but we should also find it liberating.

In fact, most people use a brutal heuristic to decide whether they like you. They don't think too hard about who you are, how you look, what you stand for, or even whether you could be valuable to know. Remember, they don't really care about you! They use a simple shortcut: *Does this person like me?*

It's that easy. If they think you're kind and you like them, they'll like you back! So, if you're concerned about what people think, act kindly, and most people will decide they like you.

Sometimes, of course, we want to be judged more accurately. For example, when I write essays and books, I need my drafts to be critiqued by a sample of friends and strangers to sharpen up the ideas and prose before publishing. I reach out and explicitly beg for truthful feedback, and when I receive their judgment, I must still reflect what is valuable and what isn't.

The author Neil Gaiman has his own rule of thumb about this: *When people tell you something's wrong or doesn't work for them, they are almost always right. When they tell you exactly what they think is wrong and how to fix it, they are almost always wrong.*

To ask for judgment is a healthy thing, but not when it's relentlessly forced on you, especially in a work environment. I worked half of my career in companies where people received very natural, frequent, and direct feedback from managers and mentors. For the other half of my career, I worked in large technology companies where every employee was judged, rated, and ultimately ranked with a score following a distribution curve, including 360-degree feedback from their peers, managers and teams they manage. This all happened every six months.

For many years, I supported the second, systematic approach, and I benefited personally, with consistently high scores and promotions. But looking back now and having reviewed meta-study data on the effects of distribution curve ranking, I'm not a fan. Most employees don't respond well to high levels of judgment and evaluation. It raises anxiety and erodes trust and creativity. It encourages them to act out of fear rather than courage. People thrive when treated honestly as humans and not when we turn them into cogs in a machine. Overall, it's only efficient for the people running the system but traumatic for those working within it.

In all these ways, the less we judge others and are judged by others, the lighter we will grow.

It reminds me of something a friend used to say: *if you want my advice, don't want my advice.*

Our energy is precious; why waste it telling others what to do? That's the world's job. If the world hasn't chosen to change them yet, why should you?

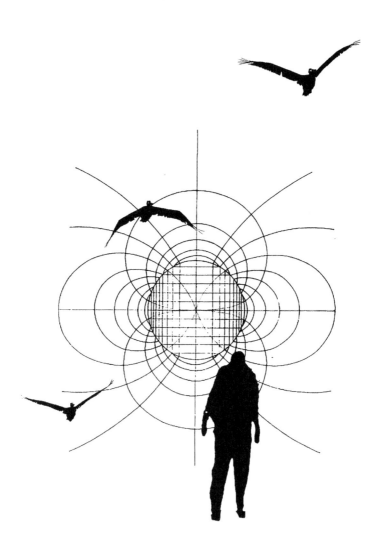

AN INTERVIEW WITH GORBACHEV, AND WHY I HATE PARTIES

"Do you suffer from any allergies?"
"Not unless you count cocktail parties."
—Richard Powers, Bewilderment

I once *almost* interviewed Mikhail Gorbachev.

It was around 1993, a few years after he'd received the Nobel Peace Prize, and I was still an undergraduate at Oxford, trying to prove myself as a journalist on the student paper. One evening, a press release came through on the fax machine. Gorbachev was coming to speak in Oxford next week, and this was my chance to get a big scoop.

I'd recently worked out that getting interviews in Oxford was easier than I'd imagined, and I was already pestering every poor A to C-list celebrity who was unfortunate enough to visit the city. I called their PR team and asked to interview them, and they inexplicably said yes and proposed a time to meet in the Randolph hotel lobby. In fact, I was on a roll. A chubby George Best dressed in an improbably pink shell suit. A very witty and kind Eddie Izzard. The dub poet Benjamin Zephaniah, over tea and biscuits served by his mum at his home in East Ham. And even Bob Hawke, the former Australian prime minister and Rhodes scholar, who held the world record in the 1950's for drinking a yard of ale, a legendary 11 seconds.

Gorbachev would cement my reputation as a serious interviewer.

I simply needed to dial the number on the fax sheet in my hand before anyone else had the same thought, and ask politely. Gorby and glory would be all mine. As I called the number, I didn't recognize the name or organization on the fax — Rabbi Shmuley Boteach, of the Oxford University L'Chaim Society. This was still five years before Google, so I was not aware that Boteach, named by the Washington Post as the most famous rabbi in America, had been sent and funded as an emissary to Oxford to raise the profile of the Chabad Jewish community, and had founded the L'Chaim Society in 1989.

I didn't know any of this. In those analogue days if you didn't know something, you just dialed and blagged it:

— Hi, is this Rabbi Shmuley Boteach? This is James Chadwick, from the Oxford Student. I understand the L'Chaim Society is bringing Gorbachev to speak next week. I'd love to interview him.

Long silence.

— Hello?

Another long silence.

— Tell me, Mr. Chadwick, why should we let you meet one of the greatest political figures of the twentieth century? What are your motivations for this interview? What relevant experience or geopolitical insight do you bring that qualifies you for this honor?

I explained about Eddie Izzard and George Best, omitting

the part about the pink shell suit.

— Mr. Chadwick, I do not know these people. Do you understand what the L'Chaim Society is, and what we stand for? Are you aware of what's happening in Israel? Have you done *any* research into us, Mr. Chadwick?

Another long silence, this time mine.

— Look, why don't you come over, and we will discuss this further? Come to my house this evening, we are having a little party. It's very informal. You can meet some of our student community and we can see where it goes. See you at 7.

The call ended, and my bowels churned a little. Fuck. This was a big problem. I desperately wanted to interview Gorby, and my future career might depend on it, but there was now a monstrous obstacle I would need to tackle first.

My deepest, darkest nemesis: A party.

I've always hated parties. I think I'm a sociable and chatty person in regular life, but for whatever reason, gatherings intimidate me. All my physical and mental faculties turn to undependable blancmange between the moment I step in and stumble out. Usually, I RSVP yes and then never get off my own sofa; a habitual no-show. On the disastrous occasions that I attend, I seek out the dullest and most isolated person in the room and monopolize them until even they find an excuse to leave early.

I'm like a colon cleanse for party hosts.

But this was for Gorby. Tonight, I needed to step up and bring my A-game. So a few hours later I was cycling through the cold, dark rain towards the Rabbi's house, hungry and thirsty for Dutch Courage. I chained my bike in the rain and knocked on the door, which was opened by a towering, elegant American girl in a black cocktail dress and pearls.

Presumably, they were her informal pearls.

—Come in, you're late; we're just getting started, she said.

My only jacket was a giant Russian army surplus coat, which she reluctantly took and hung on a tiny hanger before leading me into the living room. Things had started badly and got worse.

When it comes to groups, for me, size does matter. As Jordan said in The Great Gatsby, "I like large parties. They're so intimate. At small parties, there isn't any privacy." I hated small parties the most. I stepped into a living room with a dozen preppy, intense kids, trained in the dark arts of professional mingling, and there was nowhere to hide for the next hour. It was like being locked in the green room before the National Debate Club or Spelling Bee televised finals. One by one, they rotated in to start a conversation with me, quickly established my profound ignorance of Middle Eastern politics, and then glided out effortlessly. They just kept coming.

I was like a new lamppost that every dog in the park had to piss on a little.

Fortunately, there was alcohol, and someone kindly filled our wine glasses. Or at least someone kept filling up *my* glass. The first rule of being a British student is never to refuse free alcohol, but these American kids clearly hadn't got the memo.

More fool them, I thought.

After an hour of being a lamppost, we all moved into the dining room for a sit-down Shabbat dinner, and someone seated me opposite the Rabbi. The second rule of being a British student is to consume as much free food as possible when available, and

I took this rule very seriously. I surveyed the generous feast and set about gorging myself comprehensively. Winter was coming, and I needed to store calories. Conveniently, I was also seated in front of the only alcohol on the table, an unopened bottle of cheap vodka, so I naturally began to reapply the first rule. I decided to focus on the food and drink tasks first, and then move on to buttering up the Rabbi.

This party was all right. I was doing well. I was even, dare I admit it, enjoying myself.

Then the speeches started.

I wasn't expecting this. The Rabbi said a few words about the significance of Shabbat, possibly spoke some Hebrew, and nominated one of the preppiest kids to 'say a few words'. This kid stood up, thanked Rabbi Boteach, launched into a beautiful, sincere, witty, profound meditations on the meaning of love, raised a glass to propose a loud 'L'Chaim' toast, and smugly sat down.

What just happened? How did he do that off the cuff, I wondered, as I gave myself an extra little 'L'Chaim' with the cheap vodka? *Can all American kids do this? Very impressive.*

Next, he called up the statuesque girl in the pearls. OK, we're doing this again. She was even better! She nailed her meandering meditation on peace. Incredible. "L'Chaim!" Again and again, moving around the table, everyone killed their little speech. I still remember they had this great technique where they started with a sweet and touching observation:

— You know, Rabbi, the other day I was walking to my lecture, and I noticed two butterflies dancing in the rose bush, as colorful and happy as I've ever seen.

They'd somehow connect it up to peace in the Middle East, and we'd all shout, "L'Chaim!"

God, this was fun!

— James, why don't you share some words?"

That's funny, I thought, one of them is also called James. This should be a good one. I looked around. Why was everyone looking at me? Why was the Rabbi smiling at me?

Oh dear.

Looking back now, thirty years later, I still can't believe I hadn't worked out that my turn was coming. I knew I was being checked out for the Gorbachev interview. Almost everyone else had spoken, and I'd had my share of food and drink at their table. Ok, I had drunk rather more than my share of the wine and vodka, and I suspect that played a factor in what happened next. I remember rising to my feet and looking everyone earnestly in the eyes, long before I had worked out what to say. In fact, I'm not sure I ever planned what I said.

Unlike the American kids, I had no experience of talking in public. I had never been invited to stand up and start riffing on butterflies and my dreams for a better world. At school in England, we sat alphabetically and wrote essays for twelve years, between rolling about in the mud, singing hymns, and exploding test tubes. At no point were we encouraged to speak, let alone string together sentences. All I could remember was what my dad had once told me about public speaking: *start with a good joke; tell 'em what you're going to tell 'em; tell 'em; tell 'em what you told 'em; then sit down.*

So I did that:

— Thank you, Rabbi Boteach. Friends, I am going to tell

you a joke. How can we be sure that Jesus Christ was Jewish?

Anybody? Nobody?

— Because he lived at home till he was thirty, his mom thought he was the son of god, and he thought his mom was a virgin. That is the joke I have told you. Thank you.

I sat down uneasily. In the movies, this was the part where there's a long silence, and suddenly everyone breaks out into uproarious laughter. Or the Rabbi starts with a giggle, a chuckle, and then it ripples out from there, ending in uproarious laughter. And perhaps they would all start chanting "Gorby! Gorby! Gorby!".

But that didn't happen. Only the long silence bit happened.

I recall little after that. After the speeches finished, I tried to catch the Rabbi's eye, but he didn't seem in a buttering mood. I like to think I thanked everyone and made a polite excuse to leave, but it's equally likely that I grabbed the vodka and my Russian trench coat and cycled off into the wobbly darkness, my face burning red from the shame and alcohol. I may also have been hit by a large, wet bush traveling in the other direction, judging by the condition of my wheel spokes the following day.

Despite my hangover, I woke up early and called to follow up. An assistant regretfully informed me that Gorbachev would only have time for 'Tier 1' interviews. I crawled back into bed to wallow in vodka-soaked shame and self-pity. Fuck. No Gorby. No career. No future. All hopes were dashed by my old nemesis: a party.

I eventually got over the hangover, but I never interviewed Gorbachev. Shmuley Boteach grew the L'Chaim Society into a vibrant and controversial debating and public speaking club with over 5,000 non-Jewish members until it closed in 2001. He became close friends with Michael Jackson, and excerpts from his best-seller *Kosher Sex* were serialized in Playboy. He's written over 30 books and is still often on TV in America.

Decades later, I still mistrust parties. I can see how they once served a purpose before dating apps and Netflix, but now it seems like something we do without knowing why we still do it. But at least I don't fear them anymore. Admittedly, I rarely get invites these days, but if I did, I would be ready for them.

First, I don't care what anyone thinks of me anymore, which helps. I'm not selling myself or any services now, and I'm not searching for a perfect life partner, so it's easier to show up and be myself. Second, I've discovered that almost everyone else hates parties as much as I do. The world seems to be made up of two types of people. Introverts who hate parties outright. And extroverts, who love to tell you that deep down they're introverts but then proceed to dance semi-naked on bar tops wearing feather boas.

Finally, over the years, I have collected all kinds of eclectic advice about how to make the most of parties. I'll probably never use them myself, so I offer them up here for you to try at your next party. Enjoy!

— Find someone you don't know well, start a conversation, and then lean in close and whisper, "I just want you to know that I personally don't have a problem with you being here…"

— Instead of bringing the best-looking-but-most-affordable wine you think you can get away with, just bring ice to house parties. There's never enough.

— If someone tells you a story you've heard before, you have two choices. Option one, you immediately interrupt with an over-the-top reaction and cut it off at the pass with, "Oh yes, that was totally (insert adjective). I couldn't believe it when you told me." Option two, if you don't act fast enough, you must endure it all again, and react appropriately throughout

— Never congratulate a pregnant woman unless you can literally see the baby's head emerging. Not worth the risk.

— If someone asks you, "So where are you from?" or much worse, "Where are you *really* from?", don't waste your time getting angry about it, say to them "You go first" and keep probing until it's clearly established that we're all *really* from somewhere else.

— If you are wittier than you are handsome, avoid loud parties.

— Don't be too snobbish about hating small talk. Big people can enjoy small talk together. Small talk exists for a reason: it helps us first establish what type of person we're dealing with, and what kinds of subjects we might want to avoid. As Alain de Botton has noted, hatred of small talk overlooks that it isn't ever the subject matter per se that determines the profundity of a conversation. "There are ways of talking about death that are trivial and ways of addressing the weather that feel significant."

— Finally, as Rachel Sugar sharply reminds us, we should never tell strangers at parties who we think they look like: *"In the vast majority of circumstances, it is unacceptable to issue a verdict on the totality of someone else's appearance. You cannot walk up to a stranger at a party and declare, "Wow, great waist-to-hip ratio, but you sure do have a noticeably large forehead!" Yet that is exactly what "You know who you look like?" is, except in code."*

— Instead of asking people what they do, or where they are from, ask them if they are happy. If they're dull, they'll quickly excuse themselves.

THE TRUTH REALLY *CAN* SET YOU FREE

"There is a bidirectional relationship between truth and freedom, such that the truth will set you free, and only in being free can one aspire to uncover the truth."

— Gad Saad

I heard about this family with a dog. They'd had this dog since he was a tiny puppy, and they all loved him like they loved each other. They had young kids, and the dog spent the whole day playing outside with them. At night, he patrolled the yard and their bedrooms, watching over them. They loved this dog.

One night, the dad couldn't sleep, so he went downstairs to fix a snack. He switched on the light, and, to his horror, there on the kitchen floor was the dog with a white, fluffy bunny in its jaws. The rabbit was dead, limp, and covered in blood stains, and immediately, the dad recognized it. It was Snowy, the cute new bunny their neighbors had bought last year for their kids. His neighbors loved that bunny almost as much as his family loved their dog.

This was a disaster.

As he looked down at the blood-soaked fur, the dad started to think through all the implications. His neighbors would be devastated. This could seriously damage their relationship with them. Or even worse, what if they got the police involved? What if they demanded that their dog be permanently leashed or (the horror!) put down by a vet? His mind was racing. He had to act fast.

The dad picked up the limp bunny and took it to the laundry room. Soaking it in warm water and detergent he gently lifted out all the blood and dirt stains. Then, using a towel and hair dryer, he dried all the fur until Snowy was as white and fluffy as the day she was born. In the moonlight, he slipped out and walked over to his neighbor's yard, opened the door to Snowy's wooden rabbit hutch, and placed her back on her straw bed, fluffing her back to original glory.

He crept back to the house, mopped the kitchen floor, patted the dog, and slipped into bed. A job well done.

A few days later, he ran into his neighbor as they both returned from work and hollered his usual greeting.

—Hi Larry, how's everyone doing?

—Not good, Pete, he said, looking distressed.

—Oh no, what's up?

—The wife and kids are all totally freaked out, nobody's sleeping, everyone's having nightmares. Remember Snowy, our little bunny? Well, last week she passed away, and the kids were devastated, so we buried her in a shoebox in the yard with a little cross, and we had a ceremony, and the kids all said a few words, and eventually they got over it. A couple of days ago, little Stacey came screaming into the house like she's seen a ghost…but like a real bunny ghost…*because there, back in the hutch, all white and fluffy, but still dead, man, is Snowy!"*

I love this story because, like all great Cohen brothers

movies, everything everyone did made perfect sense at the time, yet all those rational decisions still led to a gruesome outcome.

The story also reminds us that the truth is almost always the best decision. Tiny lies can lead to outsized problems, while the plain truth will always free us.

I heard Jack Kornfield tell another story. A teenage boy in India is bedridden, and his wealthy parents are sick with worry. He can't open his eyes or move, and they've tried all the doctors and medicine they can think of. Eventually, they invite a Yogi to the house, and the spiritual man tries to cure him, but nothing works.

—This boy is very sick. As a last resort, I could try to heal him through acts of truth, said the Yogi, and they begged him to try.

—I admit that I'm not a genuinely spiritual man. I'm a fake, a fraud, and I perform these services purely for the money, said the Yogi sadly.

The boy's eyes opened. The Yogi motioned to the mother to speak.

—I, too, have something to admit. I don't love my husband; I only stay with him for the children's sake.

The boy moved and started to sit up on his bed. The Yogi gestured to the father.

—I am also a fraud, said the father with tears in his eyes. My businesses have all failed, and our family is deep in debt that we can never pay off, even though I behave like a big shot.

With this, the boy leaped into the arms of his mother and father, healed by the power of the truth.

I've never sat down to read the Bible, but its language resonates throughout our culture. We hear it in songs, movies, and speeches, and we rarely stop to consider its meaning until one day, something jolts us into deeper introspection. For me, this happened a few years ago when I came across this passage:

> *"To the Jews who had believed him, Jesus said, "If you hold to my teaching, you are really my disciples. Then you will know the truth, and the truth will set you free."*
> —John 8:31 & 32

After hearing variations of this passage all my life and watching The Matrix far more times than is healthy, I reread those six words — *the truth will set you free* — and wanted to understand them. Perhaps I was tired of hearing and telling little lies all my life. This short phrase was now demanding answers to two meaty questions. *Am I a truthful person, or at least 'truthful enough'? And how could the truth set me free?*

The first question is very personal: *Am I a truthful person, or at least 'truthful enough'?* This is rocky territory. The lies we have told for decades can become hardwired into our identity, almost impossible to parse out from who we are or from an objective truth. What if we start to unpick all those tiny threads of untruth, but we keep finding more strands, and the whole garment unravels in our hands? What if all those harmless lies have always held us together?

I can trace my relationship with the truth throughout my life, decade by decade. I don't remember many lies in my first ten years, and I'm sure my deep biases for the truth were formed then. My parents and siblings are all strong truth-tellers, and our family identifies strongly with its 'Northern roots', a sort of code in England for telling it how it is. Honesty was always the most consistently rewarded virtue at school. I remember burning with shame the day I was caught plagiarizing a poem from a book in elementary school, which suggests I rarely lied.

The next ten years were different. We moved 'down South' nearer to London and everyone in our family struggled with their fair share of secrets and deceptions. As a regular, free-roaming teenager trying to fit in, take risks, and persuade girls to fall in love with me, I became a prolific fabricator about everything I could get away with. It was part of the job description for a selfish, self-absorbed adolescent, and I'm sure I continued to act dishonestly throughout college. Of course, I wrapped it all up in a cloak of self-righteousness, but I would have lied without thinking twice in the ruthless pursuit of love and popularity.

In my twenties and thirties, trying to build a career and a family, I had to wise up. In my first job as a newspaper reporter, the radical pursuit of factual truth was drilled into me; a very helpful wake-up call. If I ever exaggerated or strayed from the plain facts, I was immediately caught out and slapped down by my sub-editors: *Just stick to the facts and keep it simple.*

In short, the adult world made it clear that truth and consistency were expected and necessary for success.

Throughout the 'heavy' years into my forties, like any parent with young children, I tried hard to balance all my roles — husband, father, colleague, manager, son, brother, friend, investor, diabolical handyman. And, of course, I struggled. Nobody teaches us how to spin plates. I consistently failed at one role or another, so I also had to learn to cope with failure for the first time. I often drank and smoked too much, and I suspect that all our friends struggling through those years together became less honest with each other and with ourselves.

It's as if we all started using tiny, habitual lies to cover up the gaps where the rugs didn't cover the floors of our lives anymore. Our little white lies that never harmed anyone: *I'll call you. I'm quitting next month. We're doing GREAT! We should get the families together. I'm on the road till Christmas. You guys are so good together!*

It was like in a movie plot when the small lies proliferate, and the character keeps running faster and faster to keep up with them, trying to hold it together.

Then, one day, in my late forties, I woke up. I was hungry again for the truth, so I started to hunt it down wherever it led me. I tried silent retreats, daily meditation, different types of books, and spending more time in nature. By gently cutting myself free from old habits, I started to understand this 'bidirectional relationship between truth and freedom.'

The logic is neat: *First, use the truth to set yourself free; then use your freedom to see the truth.* The truth will set you free, and only in being free can one aspire to uncover the truth.

Two sides, one coin.

This brings me to the second question: *"Why and how can the truth set us free?"* For most people, a more truthful life awaits them when they're ready to embrace it. The truth leads them to a calmer and more secure place, whereas lies tend to multiply and beget more lies.

Lies must generate new lies, to support themselves; the truth distills situations down to their essence.

When we embrace the truth, we can no longer suffer friends who lie deliberately or unconsciously, and we gradually avoid them. We might even find that our partners are now on a different path to us, and we need to let each other go. Love is often born out of deception and never recovers; our original lies still define the integrity of the relationship many years after the first deception.

We might also find new creative outlets to express the new truths we start to discover. This human urge to live more truthfully has inspired great art, music, and writing. "Art is a lie that makes us realize the truth, at least the truth that is given us to understand," Picasso said.

Perhaps even these essays are an attempt to find creative ways to express new truths. I ask myself questions I don't know how to answer until I read what I've written.

The truth can free us through a simpler, more creative life with good people.

But it's a process.

And if you find yourself washing and drying dead bunnies in your underwear at night, you know you still have work to do.

WATCHING ONE DAY: SIX WAYS WE MISUNDERSTAND LOVE

If you love a flower, don't pick it up.
Because if you pick it up it dies and it ceases to be what you love.
So if you love a flower, let it be.
— Osho

Just when you think you know your own taste in TV shows, a fourteen-episode Netflix rom-com pops up and gets deep under your skin. I lost a week binging *One Day*, the new bittersweet adaptation of David Nicholls's 2009 bestseller. The film tracks the long and complicated love between Dexter Mayhew (Leo Woodall) and Emma Morley (Ambika Mod).

They hook up on the final day at Edinburgh University, July 15th, 1988, and then each episode intriguingly revisits them on that same date a year later. The format is genius. It allows us to see the broad arc of a relationship over decades, especially how power shifts between friendship and love as their fortunes rise and fall. It forces us to imagine what happens between each July rendezvous.

Like a Jane Austen chapter, each episode sets fresh obstacles for their relationship — new partners, weddings, children, addiction, the death of a parent — inviting us to switch sympathies. *Who's to blame for this fight? Who's holding the relationship back now? Are we still rooting for them?*

Although they botched the final episode (Emma Morley would have hated it; way too sickly), I was hooked until then. Of course, all the British 90s nostalgia helped: a killer soundtrack, college balls, lad culture, London pubs, and getaways to Greece, Italy, and Paris. But for me, the real hook was its brutal dissection of love and how easily it can be misunderstood.

Sexy Dex and Serious Em are unlikely soul mates. They come from different places—social background, race, gender, vocation. He lacks purpose and direction, while she takes life too seriously, and there are few signs of sexual chemistry between them. Em resents the privilege that Dex was born with and his lack of self-awareness, but she still sticks with him as he loses a decade to narcissism and addiction. Their path from young to adult love in the city is messy, even brutal. Yet together, they find an equal footing over the years, and we are reminded that love is a journey, often painful and unpredictable but almost always worth it.

One Day's dialogue is knowing and sharp.

—You've never seen me before in your life, Em accuses Dex when they first meet, in a moment that foreshadows all his narcissistic thoughtlessness.

In Episode 3, Dex lies on his back while Em's head rests on his chest. In this moment, he *does* see her:

—You know what I can't understand? You have all these people telling you all the time how great you are. You know, smart and funny and talented and all that. I mean, endlessly. I've been telling you for years. So why don't you believe it? Why do you think people say that stuff? Do you think it's all a conspiracy? People secretly ganging up to be nice about you?

Soon, they grow apart. Dex finds the fame and success he lazily pursues as a TV presenter, and his ego takes over. In an excruciating restaurant scene, Dex can't stop looking over her shoulder for more exciting options, bored by her conversation, and she explodes on him outside in the alley:

—You used to make me feel good about myself. But now you make me feel like shit. Like I'm not cool enough, or interesting enough or ambitious enough.

A few years later, life begins to catch up with Dex, triggering a journey of self-awareness:

—You know, if you're 22 and fucking up, you can say, "It's okay. I'm only 22. I'm only 25. I'm only 28." But 32…

As he struggles through his thirties, they grow closer again as his marriage falls apart. When they finally get together, Em jokes "I just thought I'd finally got rid of you," and Dex tells her what she already knows, "I don't think you can." Even after almost twenty years, their love holds a mysterious power over their lives. In this moment, they simply decide to stop resisting it or trying to understand it.

If Dex and Em's lines sound familiar, perhaps it's because we've spoken variations of them ourselves. If we've loved and lost, or left and tried to return, we have likely traveled through these emotions and had these conversations. And if we've never said these words, perhaps we haven't loved yet.

SIX WAYS WE MISUNDERSTAND LOVE

The mysterious and ineffable power of love was captured poignantly eight hundred years ago by the Persian poet Rumi:

Out beyond all ideas of right and wrong,
there is a field. I'll meet you there.
When the soul lies down in that grass,
the world is too full to talk about.
Ideas, language, even the phrase 'each other'
don't make any sense.

Dex and Em's struggle to understand their love makes for compelling drama, but it also asks questions. Why does love so often overwhelm our senses? What can we expect from those who love us? And perhaps most interestingly, how do we misunderstand love?

First, *what we call love is often just starting to love.* It's falling 'in love'. We become experts in how love begins, but we know far less about how to sustain it. The first glance, words, kisses, and intimacy are preserved forever. We then long for the excitement and boundless opportunities of the first year and use them as a sharp stick to beat our relationship with in the fifth year, the tenth, and beyond. Comparing the joy of fresh intimacy with the inevitable challenge of making daily compromises is madness.

Second, *we say "I love you" when often we mean "I love love."* We crave the sense of security and excitement when in love. We crave reassurance that we are still lovable.

Third and related, *we confuse loving somebody with needing them to love us back.* If we see what someone needs, and we want to give it to them with no strings attached, that is the love that we should want. But if we only give our love in the expectation of getting the same or more back, it is something else. As Eric

Fromm writes, "Most people see the problem of love primarily as that of being loved, rather than that of loving, of one's capacity to love. Hence, the problem for them is how to be loved and how to be lovable."

When the Italians say "Ti voglio bene," sometimes abbreviated to TVB, it means "I want your good" or "I want what's best for you." TVB implies selfless, unconditional love — the kind of love we should aspire to be capable of. This love is caught sweetly in a few lines about the Sun and the Earth:

> And still, after all this time,
> The sun never says to the earth,
> "You owe Me."
> Look what happens with
> A love like that,
> It lights the Whole Sky
> —Author unknown, often misattributed to Hafiz

Fourth, *love is neither permanent nor stable*. This is perhaps the most dangerous misunderstanding to cope with. We can try to lock it up in legal agreements, ceremonies, romantic songs, and social norms, but nothing can stabilize love. The energy between two people, whose individual freedoms, wealth, urges, and dreams have been constrained, for better or worse, will always be dynamic. Love is alive, forever thriving and dying.

The only antidote is for both partners to know this and stay clear-eyed and honest about the fact that they are not the relationship. The relationship is a separate, fragile, living thing. There are always three entities involved — each partner plus the relationship itself.

Fifth, *nobody can escape the pain of being in love*. To love is to risk heartbreak, but it is worth it. Nobody can guarantee they won't hurt or get hurt, and they should doubt such promises. If our intention is to live a full life and to patiently attain a deeper wisdom, then we can expect to endure love's pain along the way:

"Oh, love isn't there to make us happy. I believe it exists to show us how much we can endure."

— Hermann Hesse

"Love blurs your vision; but after it recedes, you can see more clearly than ever. It's like the tide going out, revealing whatever's been thrown away and sunk: broken bottles, old gloves, rusting pop cans, nibbled fishbodies, bones. This is the kind of thing you see if you sit in the darkness with open eyes, not knowing the future."

— Margaret Atwood

Sixth, *we cannot hope to change somebody to love them more*. Think about the logic of even trying. You spend a lifetime searching for the right person, the perfect one, and when you find them, you start trying to polish their edges. What was the point of searching for so long if you're now planning to bend them to your own preferences? It never works anyway. It's far easier to change yourself than to try to improve someone else, and then be disappointed when they revert to who they are.

In all these ways, and many more, love is misunderstood and likely to cause suffering and heartbreak. Three essential principles emerge, though: *giving, freedom, and impermanence.* A love that is rooted in these three soils is worth wanting:

Giving is saying, 'Ti voglio bene,' or 'I want your good,' and truly meaning it.

Freedom is cutting someone free unconditionally while continuing to support their dreams.

Impermanence is committing fully to a love that is neither stable nor guaranteed.

If Dex and Em had rooted their love in giving, freedom, and impermanence, they might have lived happily ever after.

But who wants to watch fourteen episodes of happiness?

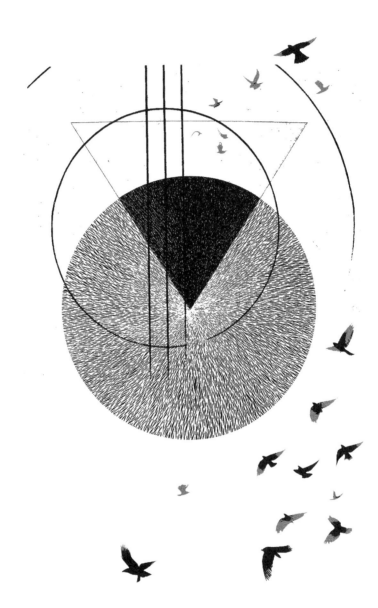

TWELVE WAYS TO READ BOOKS

"Good friends, good books, and a sleepy conscience: this is the ideal life."
—Mark Twain

Why do so many of us still read? After all, there are dozens of alternative ways to entertain or improve ourselves. Can a good book compete with a blockbuster movie or an addictive computer game? Carving out the time to sit and read alone for hours is tough; too often we lose our cherished habit.

That would be a mistake. In this essay, I'll argue for more books in our lives and share twelve different ways to read them. Some of these ideas may seem obvious, but a few might make you hungry to devour your next pile of paperbacks. To accompany the essay, I've also compiled a reading list with over 200 books across twenty genres, each with a ten-word review. You can always find it updated at jechadwick.com.

READ WITH TOTAL FREEDOM

There are too few areas of our lives that we control. Most of us wake up earlier than we'd like to, then race to hit deadlines and appointments and make hundreds of daily compromises to keep others happy. Sometimes when we live with others we don't even get to choose the movies or music we need to match our shifting mood. But nobody dictates what we read.

The books we choose and how we decide to read them are an oasis of pure freedom. Books put us in charge, allowing us to slow down and dwell on new truths or to speed past or skip tired ideas. This rare freedom is what we need more of in our lives.

Nobody can judge us for keeping five or ten different books on the go at the same time. Like tapas on a Mediterranean break, we can endlessly snack on a diet of fiction and non-fiction—Yeats on the park bench, Amis before dinner, Austen in bed.

Libraries are free and offer eBooks so everyone can access unlimited fresh books. And if you don't like your local selection, you can even ask a friend in a fancier zip code to lend you their login details.

Life is too short to slog through a dull book. If you find a book opaque or challenging to get through, it's the author's fault, not yours, so please move on. If they could think clearly, they would write more clearly, but alarmingly few do. Reading a different chapter of ten books is often more rewarding than ten chapters of one book. Modern life rarely offers pure freedom, so we must indulge in the serendipity of reading books.

Richard Powers captured this in a passage from Bewilderment: *"My son loved the library. He loved putting books on hold online and having them waiting, bundled up with his name, when he came for them. He loved the benevolence that the stacks held out, their map of the known world. He loved the all-you-can-eat buffet of borrowing. He loved the lending histories stamped into the front of each book, the record of strangers who checked them out before him. The library was the best dungeon crawl imaginable: free loot for the finding, combined with the joy of leveling up."*

READ TO BE ALONE

We can only know ourselves once we carve out time alone, and books are perhaps the best way to be alone. They provide just enough company to keep the wolf of loneliness from the door yet still demand our active introspection.

A good book gently pulls our attention between the characters, the author, and ourselves at a pace that creates space for self-compassion. Do we sometimes act like this? Are we also, perhaps, too jealous or too forgiving? Possibly. Read on.

With a day of solitude and a pile of books, we can enjoy aloneness, the welcome cousin of loneliness. In his 1905 essay "On Reading," Marcel Proust captured it well:

"With books there is no forced sociability. If we pass the evening with those friends—books—it's because we really want to. When we leave them, we do so with regret and, when we have left them, there are none of those thoughts that spoil friendship: 'What did they think of us?'—'Did we make a mistake and say something tactless?'—'Did they like us?'—nor is there the anxiety of being forgotten because of displacement by someone else."

READ TO BE INTIMATE

Our books can help us find intimacy. They open our hearts and make us available again to connect with people we might wish to love. There is perhaps nothing more erotic than to sit and read in silence with someone we desire. Books allow us to intimately experience shared meaning with other readers and invite friends and family into more profound communion. If you'll permit a borrowed pun, our books bind us. Cormac McCarthy wrote in The Passenger, "Having read even a few dozen books in common is a force more binding than blood."

Sartre once said, "I found the human heart empty and insipid everywhere except in books." Or as John Waters rakishly put it, "If you go home with somebody and they don't have books, don't fuck 'em."

Books can also have a unique physical intimacy that can last for decades. I have copies on my shelves that I swear still hold the scent of the person who gifted them to me. Impossible, right? When we find and finish a remarkable book, we should buy copies for every friend who needs to read it and insist that we discuss it as soon as they finish. Sometimes, as I read, I'm already debating who will require a copy when I'm done.

READ TO UNDERSTAND OTHERS

In Walter Isaacson's insightful biography of Elon Musk, he quotes the billionaire describing a difficult childhood:

"I took people literally when they said something…and it was only by reading books that I began to learn that people did not always say what they really meant."

My teenage fixation with Jane Austen was surely rooted in the same need to understand others, especially those new objects of desire, girls. I wanted to decode Austen's Elizabeth Bennet ("There is a stubbornness about me that never can bear to be frightened at the will of others. My courage always rises at every attempt to intimidate me.") or Emma Woodhouse ("I always deserve the best treatment because I never put up with any other.") If I could understand these 18th Century heroines' hearts, I might be more successful with

1980's girl goths. *Dear Reader, it didn't work.*

As a telling aside, Austen's novels were prescribed to shell-shocked WW1 soldiers to help them rehabilitate back into society. Following their trauma, those young men struggled to learn again how to make sense of anything. Austen helped.

Most books make us wiser somehow. Paradoxically, non-fiction reveals the most wildly improbable stories, but the most profound human truths are found in the characters of fiction.

READ OLDER, ORIGINAL TEXTS

Despite our relentless bias towards the new, the latest, the next big thing, we should fight this urge and always return to older, original texts. Books, plays, and poems can survive intact and pure for centuries, communicating ideas over the ages and revealing universal human truths. Open any battered copy of Shakespeare's complete works at a random page, and you will find fresh 400-year-old humor and insights.

The playful and erudite essayist Nassim Nicholas Taleb is insistent on the importance of older texts. He invokes The Lindy Effect, which states that the longer a non-perishable item like a book has existed, the longer it's likely to persist into the future:

> *"I follow the Lindy effect as a guide in selecting what to read: books that have been around for ten years will be around for ten more; books that have been around for two millennia should be around for quite a bit of time, and so forth."*

He believes this idea should also guide writers. If you want to write a book that will be read in twenty years, he suggests, then write a book that somebody would have read twenty years ago.

(I am trying; it's hard.)

Taleb also argues that most new texts, especially non-fiction, are disposable. No book that can be shortened survives. "To see if a book is real, ask ten people of different backgrounds & professions to summarize it," he advises. "If the summaries are similar, the book will not survive as it can be shortened to a journal article. The more the summaries diverge, the higher the dimensionality of the book."

READ BOOKS TO SAVOR THE CRAFT

We should savor all pleasures more often, such as food, music, and walks in nature. Stopping to savor is a form of meditation that usually helps to calm and clear the mind. One way to savor a book is to consider the elements of its craft. What do I mean by craft? All the author's decisions are craft: the language, pace, characters, narrative devices, dialogues, themes, story, plot, and even the typographical layout.

Whatever makes our heart skip a beat is calling out to us for a reason. Whenever we pause to consider a line or a single word choice, even if only for a moment, there's a reason. When we decide to savor a book, we notice all these atomic parts. We stop simply enjoying the story, and we begin to ask *why* questions. Books lend themselves to this form of meditation. With a movie, a play, or a piece of music, it's a moving target unless you deliberately hit pause, so it's harder to appreciate things deeply in the same way. Books invite us to stop and savor.

But don't take my word for it; try it for yourself. Here are the opening paragraphs from Metamorphosis (German: Die Verwandlung), a novella written by Franz Kafka and first published in 1915. It tells the story of salesman Gregor Samsa, who wakes one morning to find himself inexplicably transformed. It's perhaps my favorite opening passage in all literature, and I invite you to savor the writing craft and pause to spend time with anything that jumps out at you:

As Gregor Samsa awoke one morning from uneasy dreams he found himself transformed in his bed into a gigantic insect. He was lying on his hard, as it were armor-plated, back and when he lifted his head a little he could see his domelike brown belly divided into stiff arched segments on top of which the bed quilt could hardly stay in place and was about to slide off completely. His numerous legs, which were pitifully thin compared to the rest of his bulk, waved helplessly before his eyes.

What has happened to me? he thought. It was no dream. His room, a regular human bedroom, only rather too small, lay quiet within its four familiar walls. Above the table on which a collection of cloth samples was unpacked and spread out—Samsa was a traveling salesman—hung the picture which he had recently cut out of an illustrated magazine and put into a pretty gilt frame. It showed a lady, with a fur hat on and a fur stole, sitting upright and holding out to the spectator a huge fur muff into which the whole of her forearm had vanished!

Gregor's eyes turned next to the window, and the overcast sky— one could hear raindrops beating on the window gutter—made him quite melancholy. What about sleeping a little longer and forgetting all this nonsense, he thought, but it could not be done, for he was accustomed to sleep on his right side and in his present condition he could not turn himself over. However violently he forced himself toward his right side he always rolled onto his back again. He tried it at least a hundred times, shutting his eyes to keep from seeing his struggling legs, and only desisted when he began to feel in his side a faint dull ache he had never felt before.

READ TO BECOME SLIGHTLY LESS DULL

I've always felt that the worst insult is to call someone dull, and I'd be gutted if somebody labeled me unoriginal. But after living alone in a cave for 11 years, that's precisely how the British Buddhist nun Tenzin Palmo has described the human mind:

The mind rarely thinks up something fresh and new and exciting. Mostly it is just the same stale material, repeated again and again. The same old grievances and memories—both happy and sad— opinions, ideas, plans, fantasies, and fears. If we start to observe our mind, we see how unoriginal it usually is. Our ordinary conceptual mind is not really very bright.

After 11 years of solitude, she sees things as they are.

To be clear, I'm not claiming that reading more books will instantly make us fascinating. I know people who read all the best books and extract all the worst messages. But if you become a discerning reader and take the time to reflect and savor the craft, especially if you take notes and review them along the way, you should at least become less dull. The books we read still improve us even though we forget most of what we have read.

A good book is also a good conversation starter, even with

a stranger. I used to find it challenging to converse with two types of strangers: the very young and the very old. Now, I ask them what they're reading. It works well with five-year-olds and eighty-five-year-olds. And if they tell you they don't read books, you likely just saved yourself a dull five minutes either way.

READ TO GET HEALTHY

Kafka once compared books to narcotics, but all the evidence suggests they are more like tonics. Across various studies, researchers have linked books to putting our brains into a pleasurable, meditative state. Regular readers sleep better, have lower stress levels, higher self-esteem, and lower rates of depression than non-readers.

Book therapy is not a new idea. The Ancient Greeks called their library in Thebes, a 'healing place for the soul', and Sigmund Freud experimented with using literature as part of his psychoanalysis sessions in the nineteenth century. It even has a name, bibliotherapy, dating back to a 1916 article in The Atlantic Monthly, "A Literary Clinic." Bibliotherapists can refer to a light-hearted almanac of literary cures, written in the style of a medical dictionary full of lively recommendations. It's called "The Novel Cure: From Abandonment to Zestlessness: 751 Books to Cure What Ails You" by Ella Berthoud and Susan Elderkin:

> Structured like a reference book, readers look up their ailment, be it agoraphobia, boredom, or a midlife crisis, and are given a novel to read as the antidote. Bibliotherapy does not discriminate between pains of the body and pains of the head (or heart). Aware that you've been cowardly? Pick up To Kill a Mockingbird

for an injection of courage. Experiencing a sudden, acute fear of death? Read One Hundred Years of Solitude for some perspective on the larger cycle of life.

REREAD GREAT BOOKS

D. H. Lawrence once wrote, "It is far, far better to read one book six times, at intervals, than to read six several books," but I always felt he was exaggerating. Not all books are worth rereading, but a great one deserves at least three revisits over a lifetime. Perhaps as we get older, we become more efficient at forgetting, so I might return to a few of my favorite short novels six times before I die.

In the case of Hemingway's "The Sun Also Rises," Waugh's "A Handful of Dust' and Roth's "The Plot Against America", I hope so. I revisited each of them last year, each for the third time, and was struck by how different the rereading experience is from reading a book for the first time. I preferred it.

The first time we read a book, we're a little nervous. Like a first kiss, it feels exciting but awkward. Are we right for each other? Where will this go? What are we getting into? In our distraction, we miss details. Rereading is different. We already know we are in love, so we can relax. We half-remember the plot, but there are still delightful surprises. We can stop more often to savor the details, especially now that we understand the whole book. We can appreciate the breadcrumbs the author laid for us that we missed the first time.

READ TO DEVELOP A PROFOUND IDEA

Getting to a profound and unique idea takes work. There are many intelligent thinkers, and now anyone with a keyboard or a camera and an idea can publish. The world of ideas is flat and daunting. But if you read books, you have an edge. For a start, most people are too lazy to find and read the right books. Yet the complex ideas you need to build on to get to an original idea of your own are all in those books.

Remember, good books can contain sophisticated ideas, as Michael Chabon observed in his Foreword to Trickster Makes the World, by Lewis Hyde:

> *A book is a map; the territory it charts may be "the world," or other books, or the mind of the cartographer. A great book maps all three territories at once, or rather persuades us that they—world, literature, and a single human imagination—are coextensive.*

Books are the most effective medium for communicating complex ideas. Authors must work hard to distill their ideas clearly, even if only a few people read them. All it takes is to find and absorb a handful of the right books on a common theme and then synthesize and extend them into something different and better, and you can find a fresh idea. Find several books that tackle the same important theme from various angles, then write down your new beliefs.

You will also need a note-taking system to develop deep and original ideas. I've kept notes of every book I've read since 1996. Unless you combine reading with a simple habit of rereading your highlights and notes, almost everything will be lost, like sand flowing through open fingers.

READ TO TRAVEL (LIGHT)

Books and travel often satisfy similar emotional needs; they release and transport us to inspiring places. Our romantic minds link a favorite book to the warm beach or rattling train where we first sat down and opened its cover. When we revisit its pages, the sounds, smells, and stirring emotions all return.

Sadly, when we get busy with work or parenting, we can't read as often as we would like to, and our favorite pastime gets postponed to holiday reading. We store our books in a pile for the next trip. Ironically, this almost becomes the main reason to travel: to sit on the beach and read books. Yet often, by the time we've navigated flights, car rentals, and hotels, we're too tired to get through half of them.

If we're honest, we might have enjoyed our break more sitting with a bottle in our favorite chair at home with someone we love, all our devices switched off, and rereading our favorite books. In fact, with the right books, we rarely need to go far to experience many of the benefits of travel. When we travel physically, we only see tiny fragments of the world; with books there are no limits. I've traveled both ways, and there are fewer differences than you might imagine. Many decades later, the memories I still hold from reading Bruce Chatwin's 'Songlines' and 'In Patagonia,' or devouring Pico Iyer's 'Falling off the Map' or 'Video Nights in Kathmandu' are as strong as my 'real' travel memories from the same period.

READ TO STAY HUMBLE

In Alan Bennett's bittersweet play (and hilarious movie) The History Boys, Hector, the teacher, tries his best to express part of the magic of reading to the teenage boys:

The best moments in reading are when you come across something—a thought, a feeling, a way of looking at things—that you'd thought special, particular to you. And here it is, set down by someone else, a person you've never met, maybe even someone long dead. And it's as if a hand has come out and taken yours.

I sympathize with Hector. Inspiring young people to read today is tough. As a father of four boys who were once avid readers, I wish I knew how to convince them not to abandon a habit that will always provide solace. I still hope they'll return to books again as adults.

This humbling reading experience — like a hand has come out and taken yours — is essential to becoming an adult. It's the moment when we understand that we are not so special and that our pain or sadness is not so unique either, and certainly not worth losing sleep over. A good book reflects our mortality. It teases us about our pretensions and how little time we might have left. All these feelings and ideas existed before us and will continue long after us. We are not so special.

And so, Dear Reader, since neither of us is terribly special or interesting, we might as well sink into a very comfortable chair and get lost in a fresh pile of colorful hardbacks.

THE ONLY CURE FOR LONELINESS

"The reality is life is a single-player game. You're born alone. You're going to die alone. All of your interpretations are alone. All your memories are alone. You're gone in three generations and nobody cares. Before you showed up, nobody cared. It's all single-player."
—Naval

"If you are never alone, you cannot know yourself."
    —Paulo Coelho

Ten years ago, Robin Williams took his own life aged 63, and I still miss him. His loss still feels profound and personal, similar for me to losing my childhood friend, Jason, who tragically passed around the same time. Williams was perhaps the most universally loved and funniest man on the planet. His movies and actions brought joy to millions. And yet, he was deeply lonely and unhappy. He once said:

—I used to think the worst thing in life is to end up all alone. It's not. The worst thing in life is to end up with people who make you feel all alone.

Perhaps many of us still miss him because he captured the paradox at the heart of the human condition: *a day of solitude can be tragically lonely or deliciously alone, depending on how we frame it.*

In this essay, I want to explore the deep history behind this paradox of solitude and suggest a way to live more comfortably with it. When we accept that two things are equally true—that we are always and never alone—we have the foundations to embrace *aloneness*, which is the best antidote to loneliness.

But first, let's acknowledge the genuine trauma of loneliness. Loneliness is an unspoken form of suffering; without help, it can become a hole too deep to climb out of. The lonely also often experience shame that they suffer, but by definition, they have nobody to reassure them. For people whose lives are filled with the busy noise of family and friends, it can be impossible to understand and, therefore, support the lonely.

I once heard loneliness is like holding in a joke because you have no one to share it with.

But being alone does not necessarily cause loneliness, and the more we learn about the colorful history of solitude, the greater our ability to frame it positively. In early societies, humans needed to be part of a tribe. Sitting too far outside the tribal circle would mean missing the spoils of the hunt, so in a way, we are all descendants of those who chose to join and eat together at the fire. To reinforce this importance, most tribes enforced a liminal period of solitude on younger members, especially adolescent boys, as an initiation ritual to mark their transition to adulthood. Young aboriginal men, for instance, were sent out into the desert alone to fend for themselves for up to half a year. This fostered a fearful respect for loneliness and a practical tolerance for aloneness.

What does this deep history mean for us today? It might

explain why we feel anxious when we aren't invited to sit by the fire with the rest of the tribe. But it might also remind us that we are no longer so dependent on the safety of the tribe, so our primitive feelings of anxiety when alone are no longer so helpful to us. Sometimes, we must step away from the comfort of the tribe to learn to become more robust and independent. Aloneness won't kill us and can make us stronger. We grow alone.

For much of Western civilization, solitude was celebrated, and many Christian saints became famous for the long periods they spent alone. Jesus wandered for forty days and nights in the wilderness, and a strong tradition of silence and solitude was cultivated in the monasteries and nunneries of Europe. Arriving in the New World, we also fostered a reverence for the noble solitude of the frontier, as echoed in one of the most quoted passages in American literature:

> I went to the woods because I wished to live deliberately, to front only the essential facts of life, and see if I could not learn what it had to teach, and not, when I came to die, discover that I had not lived. I did not wish to live what was not life, living is so dear; nor did I wish to practice resignation, unless it was quite necessary. I wanted to live deep and suck out all the marrow of life, to live so sturdily and Spartanlike as to put to rout all that was not life, to cut a broad swath and shave close, to drive life into a corner, and reduce it to its lowest terms.

—Henry David Thoreau, Walden

This passage left a great impression on me as a teenager, like a calling to walk out alone into the world, a call from a tribal council that no longer existed but probably still should. Shortly after reading Walden in my teens, I left home before finishing school and spent over a year wandering across the Middle East and Eastern Europe. I can't say for sure that Thoreau inspired me to walk out, but I wouldn't have been the first!

In the late twentieth century, things became more complicated. Our traditional communities started to fall apart. As Robert Putnam argued poignantly in 'Bowling Alone: The Collapse and Revival of American Community':

> *The dominant theme is simple: For the first two-thirds of the twentieth century a powerful tide bore Americans into ever deeper engagement in the life of their communities, but a few decades ago, silently, without warning, that tide reversed and we were overtaken by a treacherous rip current. Without at first noticing, we have been pulled apart from one another and from our communities over the last third of the century.*

These confusing riptides surged into this century. We've continued to move into cities and suburbs, where paradoxically, we can more easily be ignored utterly in a crowd. Loneliness was already accelerating in society, and then the smartphone arrived. Our media and screens fractured into personal echo chambers, kicking away one of the last few legs that still gave us community, the 'watercooler' TV events that everyone watched together and then discussed the next day at school or work.

Social media has connected us to everyone we know and love, no matter how often or far we move around. However, it can also painfully remind us that we are missing out on a group that we didn't even know we wanted to be part of.

Ever since smartphones were launched, levels of reported loneliness, anxiety, and depression all spiked and continue to rise. Beyond parody, in desperation, the British government even appointed a Minister for Loneliness.

Looking back at where we came from — at our tribal, religious, and pioneering roots — it seems we forgot how to embrace the power of aloneness.

The response I like most is slowly increasing the quality of our human interactions while decreasing their quantity. Why quality over quantity? When we're young, we crave large groups of friends and roam around town, having more loose interactions. Perhaps more is better during this phase because we're still searching for a partner, meaning, or voice. As we age though, we often need fewer interactions. We know who we are and what will make us happy, and we might live off a few interactions a day or perhaps a week. At the same time, we crave deeper connections—to connect more authentically and openly with fewer people.

At the heart of aloneness, less is more. A single meaningful connection, combined with a routine of comfortable and simple solitude, is often all we need.

Sadly, Robin Williams never found the solace of aloneness. For the best-loved and funniest man in the world, there was always a joke he had no one to share with.

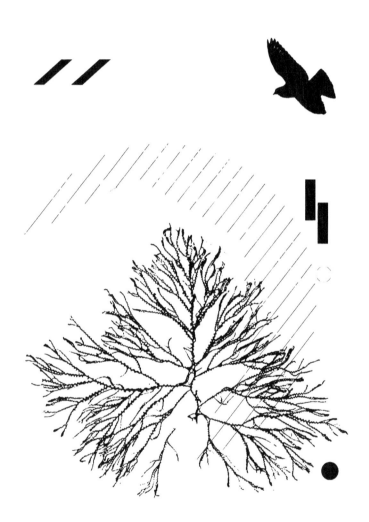

THREE WORDS TO LIVE BY

*"To try to do something which is inherently impossible is always
a corrupting enterprise."*
— Michael Joseph Oakeshott

A few years ago, we celebrated my father's eightieth birthday.
It was a low-key, modest dinner at a nearby hotel, attended by
around forty close friends and family. We ate and drank well,
played games, and gave heartfelt speeches and toasts. My
father stood up to deliver a short, humble thank you speech
and began to sit back down to enjoy his wine and dessert.

But before he could sit down, I blurted out an unplanned
question.

— Dad, what's the secret to life?

The room fell silent. For context, my father is one of the
best-loved men I ever met. He is kind, generous, wise, and
highly consistent. He was born at the beginning of World
War II, worked and saved hard all his life, survived two heart
attacks, retired, traveled, golfed, gardened, sang in the church
choir, supported various good causes, and doted on all his
grandchildren. I never heard anyone say a bad word about
him; he remains my hero and moral compass.

But I'd never asked him for the secret to life until that very
public moment, and I instantly regretted it. It seemed too personal.

Without pause, he answered — "Everything in moderation!" — then emphatically sunk the rest of his wine and sat back down.

I'm not sure anyone else recalls that moment because it was typical of his behavior and philosophy, yet it was precisely what I needed. By its own moderate logic, it required no padding or illustrations. I still don't know if he had ever thought hard about it or whether it was just a self-effacing quip.

But it was just what I needed—*three words to live by*. If those three words seem too simple and dull to be helpful, then that is perhaps the point. I suspect they contain the secret to a good life for most of us, but we are far too busy seeking the clever, dramatic, unique, and sensational. Moderation does not sell newspapers, win elections, or get Instagram followers. We spend our lives hunting for the biggest, the fastest, and the best, swinging between extremes like a pendulum. Today, it takes rare discipline to ignore the extremes and be content with life in the middle lane.

I'll share a personal story to illustrate. During my first silent meditation retreat in Java, I was confronted by my own attachment to extremes. For the first three days of the retreat, we were instructed to focus only on the sensation of the breath as it left our nostrils and touched the area around our nose, including the upper lip, for ten hours a day. This silent focus and discipline in a tiny area made us far more sensitive and receptive to bodily sensations. On the fourth day, we were guided to start mentally exploring the rest of our bodies for sensations — an itch, a pain, a hot or cold patch — one area at a time. Eventually, we were encouraged to scan our whole bodies freely for the tiniest of sensations.

This moment was explosive for me. After days of tight focus, it was highly liberating. I began to experience powerful waves of euphoric energy coursing through my body. With intense pleasure, my neck craned up to the ceiling, and my back arched. I didn't want it to stop. When the session ended, I struggled to catch my breath, and I remained afterward to approach the teacher and seek clarification on its meaning.

I was the only student who stayed back. Nobody else seemed to have experienced what I had felt. Perhaps I was unique or different? Had I found a new secret back door to happiness? I hoped so. I sat before the teacher, explained what had happened, and thanked him for guiding me to this life-changing experience.

He looked at me without emotion and spoke sternly.

— This is just your ego talking. Just focus on your breath. Please try harder to stop clinging to these emotions, both bad and good. Clinging to pleasure is no better than dwelling in your pain. Just carry on trying.

I nodded and returned to my dormitory in silence. I was deflated. I thought I'd found a magic door, but it was just my ego wanting to be unique, hunting for extremes. The goal was to stop clinging to emotions like this, even the pleasurable ones. The skill to learn was to relax the grip and to drift back to the middle. After four days of silence, I still had a lot to learn and didn't understand the simple lesson at the heart of it all:

Neither chase nor avoid things, but accept them and be there in the middle.

In our daily lives, we often feel stretched and exhausted. How do we get so depleted? Partly, we do it to ourselves by chasing extremes. Ironically, we may seek out these experiences because we believe they will 'energize' us, but the result is usually the opposite. Constantly seeking and traveling to the edges requires great exertion, even though we may not feel it. Sometimes, it can be exhausting to hold together the story of who we say we are.

But is the alternative — *everything in moderation* — enough for us? Where's the reward?

Most of us understand logically why we should live in moderation and try to 'be there in the middle.' But we don't know *the concrete benefit of moderation* until we physically experience it in our bodies. Arguably, we don't understand anything fully until we have experienced it physically. Meditation and yoga are two powerful ways to help us 'know' things in our bodies, but there are also other ways.

There's a secret reward hiding inside each of us, which we can learn to harness: energy.

When we find a balanced middle point, all that energy flows back into us. We become recharged, liberated, and, most importantly, lighter. Like a child standing at the center of a seesaw, we feel new lightness throughout our body when we choose to control the very center point.

The center is where we recover.

When we stop swinging in and out, up and down, right to left, from one extreme to another, we find ourselves balanced in the center. We are no longer hunting for the next pleasurable high and can relax our grip, allowing our bodies and minds to recharge.

We are right where we want to be: here, now, in the middle.

People often say that time is the most precious commodity, but that's only half-right. Time is worthless if you're too tired to enjoy it. The true reward is energy, which flows back to us when we find our center and keep everything in moderation.

MY FREEDOM-LOVIN' AMERICAN
TV HEROES

In the immaculate opening scene of Giuseppe Tornatore's underrated movie, *The Legend of 1900*, an ocean liner drifts silently with a deck full of fresh immigrants until suddenly, the Statue of Liberty appears above them, towering through the fog, and the desperate crowd erupts with ecstatic joy:

There was always one. One guy alone who would see her first. Maybe he was just sitting there eating or walking on the deck. Maybe he was just fixing his pants. He'd look up for a second. A quick glance out to sea and he'd see her. Then he'd just stand there rooted to the spot, his heart racing. And every time, every damn time I swear. He'd turn to us, towards the ship, towards everybody and scream... America!!!

Twenty million immigrants arrived on boats between 1880 and 1920—*the tired, poor, huddled masses yearning to breathe free*—and I'm sure most of them felt this joyful relief when they arrived safely at this colossal welcome symbol.

Land of the free. Home of the brave. *Love at first sight.*

But for me, falling in love with America took half a century, and it all started with TV heroes and superheroes. I grew up in Britain during the 1970s. Life, to play on Thomas Hobbes' quote, was *nasty, British, and short*. We had high unemployment, rampant inflation, an oil crisis, and Cold War nuclear annihilation always loomed.

And it rained a lot.

We grew up taunted by American TV shows and movies depicting happy blonde-haired kids with freckles and shiny teeth in California and Florida, hanging out on skateboards at the beach or shooting water guns in their pools. Britain was still in black-and-white, while America had already gone color. And it never rained over there.

If you were a 70's British kid, American TV was irresistibly fizzing with heroes saving the world. If you cycled home fast, ate all your vegetables, did your homework and sat quietly on the sofa in your pajamas, you could binge all your shiny idols.

There were the cop shows. Classic street-smart buddy cops like Starsky and Hutch could always be relied on to bust baddies while sliding across the hood of their red-and-white Ford Gran Torino and collecting tips from their irrepressibly streetwise informant, Huggy Bear.

One variation was *CHiPs*, short for California Highway Patrol, set on the seemingly idyllic and empty lanes of Los Angeles, which Ponch and Jon patrolled in sick Aviators and improbably tight uniforms, the color of sunlit cardboard. After busting a few baddies, each episode invariably closed with a typical SoCal activity like jet skiing with bikini girls or skydiving. The end credits would even freeze-frame, with everyone laughing together as if to make it clear how hopelessly shit our own lives were in comparison.

There were heroic American cops and detectives for all occasions. *Knight Rider* for the geeky car-lover. *Columbo* for the thinking kid. And, of course, *Charlie's Angels*, the inexplicably bikini-clad sleuths, for the lusty teenager.

The transatlantic supply of heroes was endless. There were space heroes (*Buck Rogers, Battlestar Galactica*), comic book superheroes (*Wonderwoman, The Incredible Hulk, Batman*), multiracial ethical mercenaries (*The A-Team*), and an impossibly cool but, in retrospect, disturbingly old greaser called Fonzie (*Happy Days*). There was a bionic hero, Steve Austin, in a show called *The Six Million Dollar Man*, an unfathomably large amount of money for a six-year-old in Leicester, but now barely enough to buy a townhouse in Brooklyn.

There was even a martial arts adventure hero, Shaolin monk Kwai Chang Caine, who wandered the American West in the 1870s armed only with his spiritual training and some lethal moves (Kung Fu, 1972). We didn't quite know why, but after watching *Kung Fu*, we all accepted that if a parent or teacher said, "Patience, grasshopper," we needed to chill out for a bit.

For me, the bionic eyes, bullet-proof bras, and kung fu monks were all watchable enough, but the wild and 'real' America lit my fantasies. Not the equine theatrics of *Zorro* and *The Lone Ranger*, but mountain men like *Grizzly Adams*, an innocent fugitive from the law who lived in the forest with a grizzly bear companion and rescued passers-by. Or the gritty determination of the Midwest Ingalls family in *Little House on the Prairie*.

Mysteriously, most kids' favorite show followed the antics of two cousins from Hazzard County in rural Georgia on probation for moonshine running. The Duke Boys were 'merely' armed with bows and arrows because their probation prevented them from owning guns. With their angelic cousin

Daisy, they consistently outwit corrupt sheriff Boss Hogg and greedy city slickers. Daisy's gloriously tight denim shorts — a.k.a "Daisy Dukes" — became almost as famous as the show itself, as celebrated by Katy Perry in her chart-topping 2010 single "California Gurls."

Why did *The Dukes of Hazzard* resonate powerfully with a generation of pasty British kids five thousand miles away? It certainly wasn't the political significance of the confederate flag painted on top of the General Lee, their orange 1969 Dodge Charger. And it wasn't the cameos of Country music legends who were caught in Boss Hogg's celebrity speed trap at the end of each episode and forced to sing a hit song. We had no idea who those bearded oldies were.

No, I'm convinced it was about a primitive, universal call to freedom. The Dukes are a close-knit family, living with their Uncle Jesse on a small farm in the forest. They don't have to study or work much. They have a bow and arrow and a souped-up car that can outrun and outfox the cops. They can wear Daisy Dukes. And it never, ever, ever rains.

In fact, it's all there in lyrics of Wayne Jennings' theme tune *Good Ol' Boys*, which, once heard, will jingle around your head for a lifetime:

Just a good old boys
Never meanin' no harm
Beats all you never saw
Been in trouble with the law since the day they was born
Straightening the curves, yeah
Flattenin' the hills
Someday the mountain might get 'em, but the law never will…

…Just'a good old boys
Wouldn't change if they could
Fighting the system like two modern-day Robinhoods

I hope you'll forgive all this TV hero nostalgia — I know it will mean more to some readers than others — but I think there's a point to it. America was exporting these shows at the height of the Cold War, just 25 years after the end of WW2. I'm not (quite) suggesting that the CIA infiltrated Hollywood and plotted to seduce the world with American values and iconic imagery of heroic freedom. It was likely just free-market capitalism doing its thing. But at the same time, if America *did* have a covert Cold War strategy to imbue a global generation (yup, me!) with a profound commitment to freedom and liberal values, then 1970s and 80s TV show heroes would have served them very well.

In fact, if you entertain conspiracy theories, you might reflect on David Hasselhoff's career. In the early 80s, long before *Baywatch*, he starred as superhunk crimefighter Michael Knight, the heroic driver of KITT, an (American) AI-powered gadget car. *Knight Rider* was syndicated worldwide, and its fame helped Hasselhoff become the most successful pop musician of the 80s in German-speaking Europe. Then in 1989, The Hoff released 'Looking for Freedom', which climbed the charts just as a wave of revolt began sweeping through Eastern Europe.

By the time the Berlin Wall was being hacked down, his anthem had been number one for several weeks in West Germany, with its poignant lament:

I've been lookin' for freedom

I've been lookin' so long
I've been lookin' for freedom
Still the search goes on.

On New Year's Eve, 1989, two months after the Wall had come down, Europe's future balanced on a knife edge, and America's Knight Rider was impossibly there in Berlin, spotlit and hoisted in a bucket crane above the crowd, wearing a piano-keyboard scarf and a leather jacket, singing about freedom.

Nine months later, Germany was reunified.

Had my freedom-lovin' American TV heroes saved the world once again?

HAVE YOU BEEN ANGRY
LONG ENOUGH?

"Anger is a hot coal that you hold in your hand while waiting to throw it at someone else."
— Buddhist saying.

I have an anger problem, which I'm working on.

My problem is that I rarely get angry with anybody for any reason. You could literally ram your car into the back of my car on purpose and then shout insults about my family at me, and I probably wouldn't react angrily. I've always been this way. Even during my testosterone teens, when I played rugby and drank too much alcohol, I could never muster enough anger to join a single altercation, let alone a fight.

Now, I know my anger problem is preferable to the opposite extreme. For some people, it's an uncontrollable rage that explodes exponentially and has irreversible consequences. For them, the scenario I described above might end up in actual violence and a criminal record.

I have the opposite problem, with two sets of consequences.

First, I may not get angry in the moment, but I will slowly stew about it over time. I'll experience a wave of bitterness an hour later or the next day. *What an idiot. What was he thinking? Why me?* Often, these sparks and embers grow into quiet rage. The anger is directed not just at the person who wronged me but also at myself for not doing anything about it. *Why didn't I react? Why didn't I let rip when it happened?* It might last for days or weeks. Sometimes, a spark might reignite the rage years later, and I will be angry again, far more than at the time, which makes no logical sense! I'm sure that if I had gotten appropriately angry in the first place, I wouldn't get triggered later.

The second consequence is my moral superiority about controlling anger in the heat of the moment. If I don't raise my voice or make accusations, and the other person does, I've morally 'won,' and they failed by 'losing it.' This is highly convenient when I want to avoid making compromises or sacrifices.

Which is most of the time.

I'm not talking about traumatic events like strangers driving into the back of my car; I mean all the petty disagreements and injustices of daily life. All I have to do is avoid getting angry for long enough until the other person gets frustrated and angry, invariably with my implacable calm, and then I can quietly declare victory. In my complacent view, they lost their cool and then made it personal, so I won. Given my inability to get angry during conflicts, I can play and win this game all day, which isn't much fun for those around me.

I'm working on this. I heard a valuable question a while back, and I wrote it down, which I keep asking myself:

"Have you been angry long enough?"

Sometimes the answer is yes, but usually it's no. Either way, this question inserts a valuable pause and reminds me to observe my reaction and anger. The question suggests a healthy level of anger if it's kept in check. For a long time, I felt proud that I could heed the Buddha's warning that *anger is a hot coal you hold while waiting to throw it at someone else.* It felt good not to grasp that coal and burn my hand. And it takes no effort for me. I'm doing something right for once!

But then I read the following story told by Osho, and it started to make me think differently:

> *A man once came and spat on Buddha, on his face. Of course his disciples were enraged. His closest disciple, Ananda, said to him, "This is too much!" He was red-hot with anger. He said to Buddha, "Just give me permission so that I can show this man what he has done."*
>
> *Buddha wiped his face and said to the man, "Thank you, sir. You created a context in which I could see whether I can still be angry or not. And I am not, and I am tremendously happy. And also you created a context for Ananda: now he can see that he can still be angry. Many thanks, we are so grateful! Once in a while, please, you are invited to come. Whenever you have the urge to spit on somebody, you can come to us."*

On the surface, this story echoes Jesus turning his other cheek with forgiveness to be slapped again. If the Old Testament could be distilled down to five words, 'an eye for an eye,' then its blockbuster sequel, the New Testament, might have been launched with the tagline 'turn the other cheek.' Surely, Osho's story means that we should strive to avoid anger, like the Buddha, and not be like Ananda, who could barely control his rage.

But what if there's a more valuable message in the story? A reminder to feel grateful when our temperament is tested.

Perhaps everything unpleasant that happens to us is a useful gift, *a Buddha*, a knower, or a teacher. Anger offers an opportunity to strengthen our practice, an invitation not to *follow* the heart but to *train* the heart.

Pico Iyer explores this idea beautifully in his comparison between Buddha and Jesus:

> *Buddha is a precedent more than a prophet; and where Jesus came to earth as the way, the truth, and the life, the Buddha came to suggest that the way is up to us, the "truth" is often impermanent, and the light comes and goes, comes and goes, until we have found something changeless within.*

While Jesus is presented as 'the way,' Buddha suggested that the way is up to us and always requires testing. Our goal is not to avoid anger but to experience the sparks of anger, to be grateful for their presence, and to allow them to burn a little without starting a wildfire.

There's no harm in anger that comes and gently dies. It means we care. It tells us what we are willing to fight for and gives us the energy to act.

So if you drive into the back of my car and see me talking to myself, you'll know what I'm asking:

"Have I been angry long enough?"

THE WORST SHORTCUT
TO HAPPINESS

"If you come to fame not understanding who you are, it will define who you are."
—Oprah Winfrey

I once got into an elevator alone with Samuel L. Jackson and made a complete ass of myself.

Now, I know what you're probably thinking. I didn't tell him that Shawshank Redemption was among my five favorite movies. And I didn't try to guess what the L stood for. It was arguably worse. But before I share my shameful moment, I invite you to stop reading and work out what you would have said. Imagine he looked your way and nodded, even smiled a little. What question would you ask one of the most iconic actors in the world? Or would you have respected his privacy, or frozen in fear?

The truth is, we can't easily relate to famous people as people. Tarantino once explained how fame impacted him: people just stopped talking *to* him and started asking questions. It's one of the many aspects of fame that make it the *worst shortcut to happiness.*

While many might claim that they want to be happy, they often get locked into pursuing happiness via fame. *I will first become famous for my unique talent, and then I will HAVE TO become happy.* And yet, as we'll explore in this essay, celebrity is a treacherous path to self-fulfillment. The famous forfeit a great deal of freedom, often feel empty, lose self-awareness, and attract the wrong people for the wrong reasons. This highly prized path is frequently the worst shortcut to happiness.

But first: CUT! Back to standing with Mr. Jackson, alone in the First Class lounge elevator at LAX. I had been inexplicably upgraded from Business, and he had no doubt been downgraded from someone's private jet, leaving him vulnerable to risky stalker moments like this.

At first, I decided to act cool. No biggie, I'm in LA. But the silence was deafening. Was I missing an opportunity? I must have reasoned that the safest topic of conversation would be normal, regular family chat, so I decided to play it cool.

— How's your family? I asked him.

Just three and a half simple words. Pretty common small talk. And yet, in a specific context, like, say, two strangers, one possibly a stalker or perhaps a kidnap ransom messenger, stuck together in an elevator, those words seemed to hang ominously and loudly in the trapped air far longer than the ten seconds or so that Samuel L. stood waiting for those doors to open.

Ding.

He shook his head and bolted. As that bell dinged, I resolved to find a fail-safe universal question for any celebrity encounter, which I will generously share at the end of this essay.

How should we understand fame? One problem is that I have never personally craved fame, and I've never understood those who do. Like proverbial dogs chasing cars, fame-chasers never seem to know what to do when they catch it. To be more precise and honest, I would like to become famous, but specifically for writing at least one meaningful passage that stands the test of time. And I hope to be long dead before it happens. I hope to live and die *famelessly*; to become a cult writer without ever dealing with a cult following.

People who crave fame make enormous life sacrifices to pursue it. They want it so much, they put off getting a career, or a partner, or kids or financial security. They don't just suffer for their art, they make their friends and family suffer too. Sometimes, they're so desperate for fame, even if it's only Warhol's fifteen minutes, that they take extreme risks with their lives and reputations and become *infamous* instead.

Despite knowing that the odds are heavily stacked against them and that fame is, by definition, a one-in-a-million shot, they continue to seek it.

Perhaps if they stepped back to consider how celebrities describe the experience of fame, they might think twice. Their marriages are shorter, their children struggle, and they can expect a lifetime of online abuse and stalking. In their own words, the famous are not big fans of it.

First, *fame restricts freedom*. Clive James once observed that a life without fame can be good, but fame without a life is no life at all. George Clooney described his disappointment at getting exactly what he always wanted:

> *The truth is you run as fast as you can towards it because it's everything you want. Not just the fame but what it represents, meaning work, meaning opportunity. And then you get there, and it's shocking how immediately you become enveloped in this*

world that is incredibly restricting.

Fame also clearly leaves celebrities feeling empty. Marilyn Monroe poignantly described this: "Fame doesn't fulfill you. It warms you a bit, but that warmth is temporary."

Benedict Cumberbatch also captured this emptiness: "People see a value in you that you don't see in yourself."

Or perhaps even worse, *it makes self-awareness more difficult.* Ellen Barkin notes that fame will stunt your growth, and "the younger it hits, that's when growth stops." Joni Mitchell called it a series of misunderstandings surrounding a name.

Fame also attracts the wrong kind of people. It can be fatal if a celebrity fails to learn how to choose a strong entourage. As Nassim Nicholas Taleb warned, "If you are famous, rich, or prominent, avoid people whose friends are all famous, rich, or prominent."

Fame often damages talent. Too often the first album is the best, the early novels were the most original. David Bowie managed to overcome this by relentlessly immersing himself in different art forms and reasserting his own identity. Still, he always feared the corrosive effects of celebrity. "Fame can take interesting men and thrust mediocrity upon them," he said.

In short, ask the famous: fame is no easy shortcut to happiness. *If you're searching for happiness, go straight to it; don't try to find it through fame.*

The young especially consider fame more noble than money. But why is it noble to pursue something that often fails to deliver? "You want to be rich and anonymous, not poor and famous," advises Naval. If the choice is fame or money, choose money. The world is surprisingly full of happy, wealthy people that we have never heard of, and they prefer it that way.

But perhaps most tragically, often the people who crave fame the most are least equipped to handle it. For anyone who didn't get enough love as a child and was left with a deep hole they needed to fill as an adult, fame is a dangerous way to seek completion. The type of love we all need is unconditional, but this is not what fans are offering. The adulation of a million strangers with high expectations cannot replace the unquestioning love of a parent, a sibling, a friend, or a lover.

So if your inner dog must chase a car, perhaps it should choose the happiness car, because the Ferrari of Fame doesn't seem worth catching.

I promised to share a universal question you can ask any famous person. After the Samuel L. Jackson stalker/ransom elevator debacle, I wanted a safe question in case my lips started to move again, ill-advisedly in the presence of greatness. Just six harmless words that won't get your celebrity reaching for their pepper spray. The next time you find yourself alone with your hero, try this:

"What are you working on now?"

It's polite, respectful, and almost entirely risk-free. Whatever they're currently working on is probably giving them more energy than whatever they did many years ago.

Or you can always resort to the fail-safe conversation starter that works with everyone:

"I love your shoes!"

Because famous or not, everyone likes talking about their shoes.

PERFECT DAYS
BY WIM WENDERS

Wim Wenders's movie *Perfect Days* is a simple story told quietly, creating a rare space for everyone to find meaning. For me, it revealed an unexpected and comforting truth about growing old.

The action, or perhaps more accurately, the non-action, takes place over a week or two in the life of Hirayama, a sixty-something toilet cleaner in an outer district of Tokyo. He wakes early, alone each day, on the floor of his narrow, spartan room, and rolls up his futon. The camera rarely leaves him as we follow his daily routine — brush teeth, canned coffee, drive the van, clean toilets fastidiously, lunch in the park, communal bath, street café for dinner, read under a lamp, and sleep. There is little dialogue and less storyline as he repeats his Groundhog Day, scrubbing toilet bowls until they gleam.

This could have been a soul-destroying film to endure in less expert hands. Yet, Wenders infuses every crack of Hirayama's routine with humor, beauty, and joy to create a life-affirming experience.

I watched Perfect Days last night in the theater. Before the film started, Wenders and his lead actor, Koji Yakusho, who won the Best Actor award at Cannes for his performance, gave a short introduction to thank the audience. The men stood side by side, smiling with their eyes. Wenders explained how the movie was inspired by *Komorebi* (the original title of the film), which literally means "sunlight leaking through trees," but also suggests a much larger philosophy.

Komorebi reflects the unique, almost romantic love of the Japanese for nature. It also emphasizes the importance of pausing often to notice and appreciate the tiny moments of beauty all around us. *Komorebi* is another example of a Japanese word we need in English, like *ikigai* (life value) and *irusu* (pretending not to be home when somebody rings your doorbell).

Hirayama not only understands *Komorebi*, but he expresses it through his every gesture and impish smile. At lunchtime, he sits in the park and takes photographs with an old camera of the dappled sunlight leaking through the leaves above from the same tree. Every week, he develops the 35mm film and keeps only the best photographs of his tree in a memory box. He saves tiny saplings from the parks and brings them home to nurture lovingly. Even at night, his black-and-white dreams feature shimmering branches and leaves. There's a delightful Wenders visual moment in the middle of the movie that's easy to miss. The cleaner is busy inside a cubicle polishing a toilet when he hears voices outside. He pauses and looks up to watch the blurry-colored figures of the passers-by reflected on the toilet's ceiling.

If you look for it, sunlight is always leaking through trees.

Komorebi is not only about nature, though. Hirayama carves out an analog path within an overwhelmingly digital city. He devours paperbacks at home and in restaurants, and above all, he cherishes the collection of 1970s cassette tapes in his van. These provide a loving Wenders soundtrack: Van Morrison, Otis Redding, Jagger, Nina Simone and of course Lou Reed's eponymous 'Perfect Day'.

Hirayama lives a modest life, but he is not alone and finds many small ways to enjoy human connection. He harbors a secret love for the proprietor of his favorite restaurant, and plays tic-tac-toe with a stranger he never meets, hiding a sheet of paper daily in one of the toilets he cleans. When his teenage niece turns up unannounced for a few days, he quietly gives her the calm love she needs. She can't understand why her uncle lives like this, disconnected from her wealthy mother. She wants to understand what 'her world' is, and he gently offers wisdom: "Next time is next time. Now is now," which reassures her.

This "now is now" philosophy also infused how the film was made. With no time for rehearsals, the whole shoot took only seventeen days. Yakusho didn't know that his role would be mostly silent until the script arrived; the silence puts more weight on the intimacy of the actors' expressions and movements.

The film has an interesting backstory. During the pandemic, Wenders was upset about the break-down of the 'sense of common good' in Germany, and hearing this, Koji Yanai, billionaire scion of the Japanese clothing giant Uniqlo, reached out. Yanai had launched The Tokyo Toilets, a public-private renovation initiative in Shibuya, to push the design limits for public toilets. The seventeen toilets feature designs by celebrated Japanese architects, including Toyo Ito and Tadao Ando. Yanai was angling for a short documentary, but Wenders was so inspired by the designs, including a breathtaking set of three transparent cubicles that turn opaque when the user locks the door, but also by this very Japanese commitment to public responsibility, he wanted to make a feature-length film.

Is it a realistic portrait of working-class life? Perhaps not. The toilets Hirayama must clean are far less stomach-churning than the average Japanese toilet and nothing compared to those a British or American worker might have to endure. Wenders admits: "I did idealize Japan a little bit in this movie and in this character…I'm not sure if a man like this really exists — but I think he should…Just as I needed angels to show Berlin [in Wings of Desire], I needed a caretaker for these toilets."

For me, *Perfect Days* asks an important question. It's related to *Komorebi*, noticing the everyday beauty in things, but it also goes further. The question I asked myself on the drive home was this: "Could I be happy living Hirayama's life, and if so, what are the implications of this for how I live my life today?"

I should declare that I'm 52 years old and curious about growing old gracefully. It doesn't scare me; in fact, it excites me. Just as there's an art to being young and succeeding in mid-life, there must be an art to aging well. I'd like to know it. Here in Hirayama, a man appears to be doing it well, or at least happily, and with modest means or expectations. To be even more blunt, the critical question the film asks each of us, is *how will we cope if we end up poor and alone in our old age?*

This isn't an academic question; it might happen to all of us. Hirayama has little money, few possessions, no partner or children, and must wake up early to clean public toilets. By most measures of society, he is failing. And yet he is happy.

Why is this such a critical question to ask ourselves early and often? If we believe we will be 'happy enough' in old age, even if we end up single, poor, and taking pride in a simple job, then this is useful to know now. This knowledge could console us and reduce our fear of an uncertain future. It might help us enjoy the present, knowing that even a modest retirement would still be pleasant.

As with Viktor Frankl's *Man's Search for Meaning*, the film reminds us that our greatest freedom is to choose our attitude. Frankl writes, "The attempt to develop a sense of humor and to see things in a humorous light is some kind of a trick learned while mastering the art of living."

There are, of course, no perfect days. Hirayama's face beautifully communicates this in the film's final scene, as Nina Simone's 'Feeling Good' plays on his cassette player. Every day will bring joy, sadness, strength, laughter, loneliness, and love.

Next time is next time. Now is now.

HOW TO FIRE AND REHIRE YOUR MIND

"The French have an expression for being bored—je m'ennuie—which means literally, "I bore myself." Exactly. It has nothing to do with what is going on around us. Our minds bore us."
—Jetsunma Tenzin Palmo

"It's difficult to bootstrap yourself out of the prison of your own thoughts. Essentially you must learn to think yourself out of your own mind, unchain yourself with the very chains that restrain you. The problem of knowing who you are is the problem of smelling your own nose."
—Alan Watts

I ask you to suspend your disbelief for the next five minutes to *consider the possibility that almost everything your mind has been telling you about the world has been incorrect.* This should be long enough to explore the following five ideas with me:

1. We are not our thoughts
2. We can observe our thoughts
3. Our thoughts are usually unhelpful
4. We can fire our mind and then rehire it
5. We can thrive with less thinking

First, we are not our thoughts. This should be easy to accept if you have tried meditating for just one minute. We cannot control them for over a few seconds, so how can we *be* them? They come and go as they please, flitting between the past and the future, the negative and the positive. We can all shut our eyes and try to count upwards, and most likely, we won't even reach ten, at least not without wrestling with those uninvited guests: our thoughts.

If you don't believe me, stop reading and try it for ten seconds.

Sometimes, we notice them, but usually, we don't. We don't *think* them. If anything, it's more accurate to say that *they* think *us*. When we fail to notice them, we identify with them, which is why we go along with this fiction that we are our thoughts. But we didn't invite them, we don't control them, and as we'll see, they are seldom our friends, so it's essential always to remember that *we are not our thoughts*.

Why are there so many of them? Because we develop a bad habit of using thoughts to cope with the world. We recreate the world in our minds to make it easier to understand and to give ourselves the illusion of control. We can't control the real world, so we create the world in our minds and then endlessly talk about it, mostly with ourselves! It gives us a false sense of power to classify things, criticize them, and plan what to do about them. What we call thoughts are just fragments of repeating conversations between two temporary, fictional characters, both of whom are 'us', trying and failing to make sense of our fears and cravings.

In all these ways, we are not our thoughts.

Second, *we can observe our thoughts*. Our consciousness is separate from our thoughts, and we know this is true because we can use our consciousness to focus on our thoughts. We can direct it like a stage spotlight above in the roof of a darkened theater to observe the conversations and the fictional characters talking on the 'stage' inside our heads.

Usually, we don't notice them, or worse, we identify with them. We mistake them for ourselves. But if we learn this new skill, we can use that spotlight to examine our thoughts instead of identifying with them. The easiest way to do this is to practice meditation, even for only twenty minutes daily. This is the best way to think about meditation. We find time to sit in silence and practice listening to conversations instead of identifying with them.

There's no need to judge them or censor them. Listen to them as an observer, as if we are up in that dark theater roof, with a relaxed grip on the spotlight, and note the conversation. You can't stop the thoughts from arriving uninvited, which would ruin the exercise's value anyway, but you can choose not to identify with them. Usually, it will be a familiar and tedious thought, causing you anxiety and boring you until the next idea pops up. Simply note it and wait for the next thought to arrive. Some people find it helpful to label each thought to avoid identifying with them. An example of a label might be "Too busy," or "Not talented enough," or "Anxious about gaining weight." Whatever works. This is all it means to observe your thoughts.

You will get the hang of it if you do this for long enough. In fact, after a while, you won't just be noticing the thoughts, but you'll start *noticing the Noticer*! You'll find a new location for your consciousness, somewhere 'up there' in the darkness with the spotlight, watching all the action in the theater. There's a stage where the characters are talking (thoughts), and perhaps there are stage directors or people in the audience (versions of you) watching the thoughts, but you are now up in the rafters, watching everything below with your spotlight. It should feel better to be more in control. Of course, this is not 'pure' reality; it's still a dualistic mind. But it does give us enough space to see a thought as a thought and an emotion as an emotion. At least we can choose whether it's a valuable thought or feeling. We know it for what it is, rather than being consumed by it. We no longer identify with it.

The third point is *our thoughts are usually unhelpful.* You may have read about how misleading even a healthy brain can be. Nobody writes more precisely about this than Daniel Kahnemann, whose book *Thinking Fast and Slow* outlines how our two thinking systems fight for control over our actions and lead us into errors of memory, judgment, and decision-making. "System 1" is quick, emotional, and rooted in gut instincts; "System 2" is much slower, more rational, and more considered.

It's a wise book, but arguably, you would learn more about this *deep in your bones* by observing and labeling your thoughts for twenty minutes a week. You can watch all the calories of mental energy burned by unhelpful thoughts in your brain. You will see how many negative, dramatic, and sensationalist thoughts parade on your stage, tempting you to attach to them.

Our thoughts are dull. I've always felt that calling someone dull is the worst insult. I would hate it if somebody I valued called me unoriginal. But after living alone in a cave for eleven years, that's precisely how the Buddhist nun Tenzin

Palmo has described the human mind:

"The mind rarely thinks up something fresh and new and exciting. Mostly it is just the same stale material, repeated again and again. The same old grievances and memories—both happy and sad— opinions, ideas, plans, fantasies, and fears. If we start to observe our mind, we see how unoriginal it usually is. Our ordinary conceptual mind is not really very bright."

—Jetsunma Tenzin Palmo

A high proportion of our thoughts are negative, and those negative thoughts tend to give off sparks that light new, dangerous wildfires in our minds with no apparent benefit to anybody. Thought A sparks Thought B, which sparks C and D, and so on, until we're professionally hijacked.

In short, our thoughts are usually dull and unhelpful, but we are addicted to them anyway. It's like having a highly distracting computer in our brains, which is running someone else's program from a previous era. Or having a long-running TV series we love running on repeat. I love *Seinfeld*, but there's more to life than watching reruns.

This brings us to the fourth point: *we can fire our minds and rehire them to do a simpler job.* This proposal should not be controversial, given how unhelpful our thoughts are. However, somehow, cutting them loose still makes us uncomfortable. Logically, if most of our thoughts are unhelpful, shouldn't we try to live without them? Yes, we should, but it feels daunting and unnatural to learn the alternative way, which is to think less. To think less sounds heretical. Especially in the West, we have elevated rational thinking and logic to such a preeminent status that it seems odd to try to think less. And how would we even start?

One way to start, as Michael Singer describes it, is to fire the mind from the way we are using it today:

Einstein used his mind to ponder "thought experiments" about the behavior of light, gravity, and the physics of outer space (even though no human had ever been there!). Meanwhile, you keep your mind busy with relationships, what people think of you, and how to get what you want and avoid what you don't want.

and

You have given your mind an impossible task by asking it to manipulate the world in order to fix your personal inner problems. If you want to achieve a healthy state of being, stop asking your mind to do this. Just relieve your mind of the job of making sure that everyone and everything will be the way you need them to be so that you can feel better inside. Your mind is not qualified for that job. Fire it, and let go of your inner problems instead.

—Michael Singer

Once you've fired your mind from what it was doing (badly), you can now rehire it for another task, one that is more aligned with what you want to achieve. Perhaps that's quantum physics. Or writing beautiful songs. Or helping someone that you love. Or observe your thoughts and 'notice the noticer' instead of identifying with the thoughts themselves. The main goal is to be intentional about whatever job you're hiring your mind to do for you so that it stops doing the unhelpful job it was doing before.

Fifth and finally, *we can thrive with less thinking.* We know this is true because we have all experienced *flow* at some point. Flow is when we are doing something that we do well and enjoy doing, and we become lost in the activity because there is no need to think. It's different for everyone, but we instinctively know what gives us flow. It might be a sport, music, painting, making love, or fixing a car engine. We can change our lives to spend more time doing these things and less time thinking.

When we fire our minds, we can rehire them to find flow.

We thrive when we find our flow. If it's fun, it's probably flow. We are more likely to find flow with people we love, especially when serving others rather than ourselves. We find it doing something physical, outside in the sea or up a mountain, because as a species, we have been animals that move and act for far longer than we have been a species that worries about deadlines and communicates complex concepts to each other.

Overthinking exhausts us; we should do it only when required for a specific purpose and only with a clear, calm mind. The more we can give ourselves the space and permission to empty our minds and let go of the unhelpful thoughts, the fuller our lives can be.

Empty mind, full life.

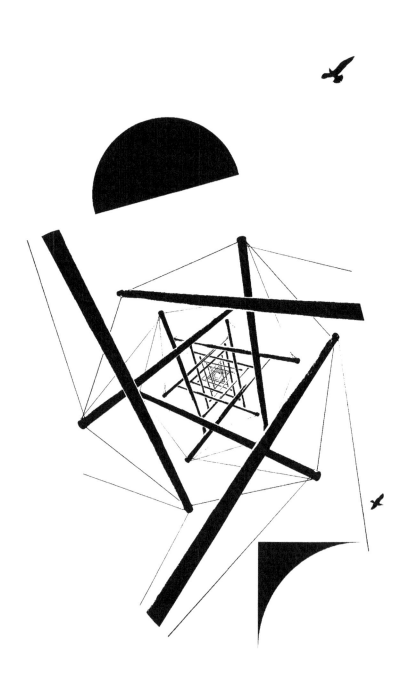

DOES YOUR INNER VOICE
HAVE A VOLUME DIAL?

"All men need enough solitude in their lives to enable the deep inner voice of their own true self to be heard at least occasionally. When that inner voice is not heard, when he cannot attain the spiritual peace which comes from being perfectly at one with his true self, his life is always miserable and exhausting"
—Thomas Merton

A man walks into a monastery. He takes a vow of silence and commits to speaking only two words every seven years. After seven years, the monks summon him and ask him to speak.

"Hard bed," he says. They nod and dismiss him.

Seven years later, they summon him again.

"Bad food," he whispers. The monks all nod and wave him out.

Seven more years pass, and they bring him back.

"I quit," he declares.

This time, the abbot can't control himself.

"Oh, big surprise!" he says, "You've done nothing but complain since you got here."

The longest stretches of silence I ever experienced were ten-day Vipassana retreats. The lack of human communication makes you feel disoriented for the first few days. Nobody talks to you, nor do you talk to others, which means you no longer spend energy trying to interpret or perform all those endless stories.

At first, you miss the human reinforcement that you *exist*, but after a week or so, you start to enjoy this new, quiet freedom. Then, you start noticing a new, quieter soundtrack. There's no TV, music, arguments, podcasts, gossip, ringtones, or keyboard tapping. In their place, there's a new background hum of birds, insects, wind, streams, leaves, and the gentle shuffle of fellow meditators as they struggle with their positions.

It's delicious. It was always there, but you never noticed it before, and now it feels like someone silenced the other soundtrack and raised the volume on this one. Finally, on top of this soundtrack, there's a new noise to get used to: your inner voice. It was also always there, of course, chattering away with itself in the background, but you have become an expert at drowning it out with playlists, screen time, and Netflix episodes. But here you have no defense. You are forced to listen to it for around sixteen hours a day, and hopefully, with the gentle guidance you are given each day, you are also learning how to observe it rather than identify with it.

We start asking ourselves a new set of questions about this inner voice. What will we learn about ourselves? Will we cope with listening to it all on our own? And why did it take us so many decades to sit down and finally listen to it? What were we afraid of?

And then, for me at least, we start asking this weird new question: *Does my inner voice have a volume dial? And if so, what default level is it set to?*

Before you read on, with your own inner voice, please try to answer yes or no.

So, it turns out *it does*—or at least mine does. I didn't know this until I noticed on the retreat that my inner voice was practically shouting at me, and I could barely hear the delicious background noise of the meadow outside the room.

For the first time, I wondered if I had a volume dial. I tried to change my inner voice to a whisper instead of full volume, a "3" instead of a "9." Unbelievably, it worked immediately, and for the rest of the retreat, I was able to observe my thoughts in a softer whisper that was far more enjoyable to listen to.

It was quite a revelation. I always knew that I had the power to move to a quieter place and meditate, but I didn't know I also had volume control for my inner voice. It made me feel even more in control of my mind than before. I would have never known this if I hadn't stepped out of daily life to change my soundtrack. It was another reminder that we can change the volume in our lives to make ourselves feel lighter.

Why don't we do this more often? Tenzin Palmo, the remarkable British Buddhist nun who lived for eleven years on her own in a cave in India, believes we are afraid:

"We are afraid of silence—outer silence, inner silence. When there's no noise going on outside we talk to ourselves—opinions and ideas and judgments and rehashes of what happened yesterday or during our childhood; what he said to me; what I said to him. Our fantasies, our day-dreams, our hopes, our worries, our fears. There is no silence. Our noisy outer world is but a reflection of the noise inside: our incessant need to be occupied, to be doing something."

— Tenzin Palmo, Into the Heart of Life

Starting to listen to your voice again is both delicious

and deeply human. You sense you were born to listen attentively to yourself, but somehow, you forgot how to do it. Biologically, this makes sense because we are human apes, just a few hundred generations from a society where the ability to listen to the signals and chatter of the jungle or the savannah would determine whether we would eat or get eaten. Especially in America, even a few generations ago, people lived right on the frontier between the city and the unknown, between the noise we created and the noise from which we came. It was essential to pay close attention to threats from the wilderness.

I often have this urge to go outdoors and be a listening animal. In nature, even silence seems loud; the quieter you are, the more you can hear. One reason our family decided to move to Utah was to spend months of the year in the mountains because the easiest place to find total silence is on a mountain alone in the snow. I first experienced it while trekking in Nepal, and I've sought it out ever since. Whether you walk out in the backcountry or up a chairlift on a quiet day, the silence is uniquely deafening. Peter Matthiesen, the enigmatic writer, zen teacher, and onetime CIA agent, captured it beautifully in *The Snow Leopard*:

> Snow mountains, more than sea or sky, serve as a mirror to one's own true being, utterly still, utterly clear, a void, an Emptiness without life or sound that carries in Itself all life, all sound.

If you don't have a mountain to hand, a unique way to explore the experience of sitting silently together might be to attend a Quaker meeting, which take place all over the world. Formally the *Religious Society of Friends*, the Quakers or 'Friends' date back to the English Protestant movements of the 1650s and offer a very personal and quiet form of worship. Here's how they describe their meetings, which are open to all and often held at local meetinghouses on Sunday mornings:

> *A Quaker meeting is a simple gathering. Because Friends believe that Spirit may reveal itself to anyone, we don't have priests dispensing grace to a congregation of followers; instead, everyone arrives at the meetinghouse as equals, and seating is usually arranged so everyone faces each other in a square or a circle. Then, in what's known as an unprogrammed meeting—because anyone could be the instrument through which God (or Spirit, if you prefer) chooses to give a message—everyone sits in silence, usually for an hour, and waits to see if a message comes.*

For a more active, transformational experience, many people travel to France and Spain to walk the Camino Way in silence. Pilgrims travel from all corners of the world to silently walk the Way of Saint James, known in Spanish as the Camino de Santiago, the almost 500-mile path from Saint-Jean-Pied-de-Port in France to Santiago de Compostela near the western coast of Spain. The early pilgrims deliberately traveled slowly, forgoing the use of river barges or horses in favor of their own feet. A pilgrimage from northern Europe to the remains of St James in Santiago could take eight months, with travelers leaving in the spring and returning in the winter.

It's now at the very top of my bucket list, and when I walk the Camino Way, I plan to carry the poetry of David Whyte, either in my backpack or my head, and especially this verse:

FOR THE ROAD TO SANTIAGO

For the road to Santiago,
don't make new declarations
about what to bring
and what to leave behind.
Bring what you have.
You were always going
that way anyway,
you were always
going there all along.
—David Whyte

Escaping noise also helps us with creativity. When we sit alone to create something — perhaps to paint or to write — we need to hear ourselves clearly, and silence creates a space that must be filled. As Aristotle understood, nature abhors a vacuum. Marcel Proust, who gave us *A la recherche du temps perdu*, perhaps the most intimate (and longest!) portrait of an inner voice in all of literature, apparently lined his walls with sound-absorbing cork, closed the drapes, and wore earplugs. He knew that great work comes from great silence.

In all these ways, then, we can choose to turn down the volume and listen. We can switch off our devices, walk silently, find snow, pray, or meditate. When we take the time to find our own volume dial and turn it right down, we regain some control over our thoughts.

We give ourselves the chance to listen and perhaps, from this quieter place, even to create again.

THE DAY YOUR EGO DIES

*"You don't kill your ego; you kill your identification with your ego.
As you dissolve into love, your ego fades. You're not thinking about
loving; you're just being love, radiating like the sun."*
— Ram Dass

On the final day of a Vipassana meditation retreat, there is
an awkward and unique moment when the curtain of silence
is lifted. All the students are invited to communicate again
after ten days of total silence, and nobody is quite sure how to
begin. On the one hand, we feel deeply connected to this new
tribe of strangers, having sat, eaten, walked, woken, and slept
together. At the same time, we feel reluctant to talk again,
afraid that we'll say precisely the wrong thing, and anxious
that all the important work we've done to calm our minds and
to tame our ego will immediately unravel, and all the effort
will have been wasted.

*What if we open our mouths, and the same self-centered storytelling
babbles out? Perhaps our minds can only be calm here, on retreat, and
not in real life.*

So when, at the end of my first retreat in Idaho, we all sat
down on the grass in the sun, and I found the courage to talk
again, I hoped that I would notice a positive change.

Nope.

Within a few minutes, I had explained to the whole group what an incredible guy I was. My first few stories included my most positive talking points: my talented sons, career, and education. My ego had reasserted itself with a vengeance.

As I climbed into my truck and headed back down the mountain for the long drive home, I started burning up with shame. For an hour, I felt more lost than ever. Had I just wasted eleven days and made no progress? I was re-entering the churn of daily life exactly where I left it. My ego was still out of control and calling the shots. After a hundred miles of driving, I managed to catch myself and could see *how my thoughts were thinking themselves.*

I decided to stop and walk for a while before going home. Something was different. Although my ego had reasserted itself aggressively, at least this time, I had noticed it, and it felt all wrong. This ability to observe the power of my ego asserting itself suggested that I was more detached from it. And sitting on the grass, I was not the only one telling my stories. Most of our egos were bubbling away like hot lava flows, finally released after forced repression.

Perhaps I had learned something after all, made some progress, and the retreat had not been a waste of time.

This gentle struggle with my ego suggested several new questions: *What is ego? Why are we so attached to it? How does this attachment hold us back? How can we learn to let go? And most importantly, what might it feel like to break free from the ego gently?*

Starting with *What is ego?* Most simply, our ego is the self, contrasted with another self or the world. It's tough to step out of oneself and observe ourselves. When we assert it, the ego acts like a mental cage that we build around us to keep others out and trap ourselves inside. We then sit inside our cage, looking out at the world as something separate from us, often unhappily. Even when we realize we are inside this cage of ego, we might still blame others for imprisoning us. Then, we give ourselves the task of changing it, extending it a little, or breaking free from it.

Was there a time when we were truly free from our ego, 'before the cage'? It's hard to remember back that far. We might see children playing, and we can faintly recognize and recall when we didn't feel separate from others and the world around us. But the ego always powerfully reasserts itself, like a prison we built many years ago and then forget why.

The second question is, *Why are we so attached to it?*

Partly, it is deep in our genes. Humans are not wired for happiness; we are wired for status, and the ego is where we locate it. Our ego attachment is rooted in fear, perhaps the fear of not being enough, of being unlovable, of dying without being noticed or making a mark on the world.

Perhaps there's also a cultural context to this attachment. I've lived in Europe, Asia, and the USA, and the differences are revealing. I grew up in the gentle Church of England protestant tradition, where it was encouraged from an early age to develop a personal relationship with God and to take full responsibility for making your way in life. I've also lived in the mountains of the American West, where rugged individualism is celebrated on every truck's bumper sticker. However, I spent the first two decades of my career working across a dozen Asian cultures, where most people are raised to keep their egos firmly in check, somewhere in the background, as Yiyun Li captures neatly:

A word I hate to use in English is I. It is a melodramatic word. In Chinese, a language less grammatically strict, one can construct a sentence with an implied subject pronoun and skip that embarrassing I, or else replace it with 'we'. Living is not an original business.

In the West we are encouraged to assert our differences early on or risk fading into obscurity. If we have siblings, we must remind the rest of our family how we are different from them and, therefore, require special attention. If we don't speak out for ourselves in the classroom and at work, we are told, then nobody else will do it for us. To get grades and enter college, students are increasingly forced to write personal statements, exploring new identities, which are read out to the class for applause and unequivocal affirmation that they are different and unique.

In the West, our ego gets graded.

Unsurprisingly, we believe we are an essential center of the universe, at least *our* universe. If we stay right there, calling the shots and asserting our ego, we can keep holding ourselves together, remain in control, and make all the right decisions. Not only do we become firmly attached to our ego, but we are attracted to the egos of others. From an early age, we find ourselves attracted to whoever has the loudest ego in the room. Anyone with a 'big ego' seems to keep winning.

Hell, they might even become President!

The louder they become, the more friends, attention, followers, dates, and prizes they get. With teenagers, there's an unofficial ego arms race where the most extreme behavior grabs even more attention. Things start to get out of control, with the demands of the individuals overtaking the sense and unity of the group.

Looking back later in life, it all seems like madness. Why were we once so attached to our egos and attracted to the extreme egos of others? As we age, the world teaches us tough love lessons; our own egos tend to recede, and we become more sensitive to others' egos. We learn to prefer spending time with lower-ego people because they create a quieter space between them and us, where we can also exist and a meaningful relationship can take root. Through the gentle feedback of the world and others, we no longer need such a strong ego to survive and thrive.

The third question is, *how does our ego hold us back?*

The metaphor of the ego as a cage can again help us here. When we look out from our cage, we are stuck experiencing ourselves instead of experiencing reality. From our cage, we develop strong ideas about where we can and cannot go and who we can become. We develop fixed expectations about how the world should see us and become frustrated when others refuse to see us correctly. We become attached to the possessions and belongings in 'our' cage, thus projecting our sense of self onto things that are not us and developing fear about losing those things.

We develop dozens of habits in our cage to occupy our time, so we don't think about the cage itself. If we can fill our hours with screens, books, podcasts, friends, shopping, sex, exercise — just about *anything* — then we might live happily inside our cage and not have to deal with what lies outside it.

Fourth, *how can we learn to let go?* I find it fascinating how many people recoil at the prospect of letting go of their ego. They equate losing their ego with losing their soul, their identity. Something so aspirational to some – shedding our burdensome ego – can clearly terrify others.

To let go of our ego, we must look inward. When the Dalai Lama was asked how to end all wars, he suggested we might start by resolving the conflicts in our lives first. Krishnamurti suggested that to listen, one must have an inward quietness, freedom from the strain of acquiring, and relaxed attention. For the Indian sage Ramana Maharshi, the spiritual path meant to ask himself three questions persistently:

Who sees when I see? Who hears when I hear? Who feels when I feel?

How might we learn to let go and gently detach from our ego? One idea proposed by Bertrand Russell is to gradually immerse yourself in ideas and interests that are far more universal than you will ever be:

Make your interests gradually wider and more impersonal, until bit by bit the walls of the ego recede, and your life becomes increasingly merged in the universal life.

Meditation and spiritual practice can help, but they can also lead us towards even stronger egoism, as warned by Tenzin Palmo:

Egoism can easily take hold of our spiritual practice. We may study the Dharma, do practices, and go to teachings and retreats, but all can become means to enhance this sense of I: I am a spiritual person; I have read so many Buddhist books; I have met all the best lamas; I have received all the main empowerments; I do important things at my Dharma center; I am special.

Perhaps the easiest way to detach from the ego is by love, or 'becoming love' as Ram Dass put it:

You don't kill your ego; you kill your identification with your ego. As you dissolve into love, your ego fades. You're not thinking about loving; you're just being love, radiating like the sun.

For many, this finally happens on the day we become parents. In his angst-ridden letters, Franz Kafka longed for the day when the burden of his ego might transfer from himself to a child.

Alain de Botton also explores this idea:

We learn, too, that being another's servant is not humiliating, quite the opposite, for it sets us free from the wearying responsibility of continuously catering to our own twisted, insatiable natures. We learn the relief and privilege of being granted something more important to live for than ourselves.

This brings us to the final question: *What might it feel like to gently break free from our ego?*

Evidence suggests that *joy* is part of the answer. When we encounter deeply spiritual and ego-free souls, they always seem to be full of joy. *Mission: Joy*, a beautiful book and award-winning film about the lifelong friendship between Archbishop Desmond Tutu and the Dalai Lama, illustrates this perfectly. There is laughter, lightness, and warmth for everyone around them.

The film reveals the ultimate reward for living a compassionate life. Once freed from ego, both men have all the time in the world for others. The past and the future have no meaning when the present is so rich.

The absence of ego, it seems, leaves only joy.

ABOUT THE AUTHOR

J. E. Chadwick is a British-American writer and father of four boys, living in the snowy bit of Utah. His novel *Path: A Story of Love, A Guide to Life* is a boy-meets-girl story featuring Buddhist teachings and thirty illustrations by his son Lawrence. Chadwick publishes weekly Substack essays at *Like A Bird*, exploring culture, books, and Vipassana meditation.

Chadwick quit school to hitchhike across Europe and the Middle East, where he rented snorkels in Israel and ran a guesthouse in a Turkish cave before studying English at Oxford University and working in media for thirty years.

More at jechadwick.com.

Also By J. E. Chadwick

PATH: A STORY OF LOVE, A GUIDE TO LIFE

"*Path* is a journey to the heart of what matters...its message reminds one of *The Alchemist*. Powerful and poignant."

—James R. Doty, M.D., author of the New York Times bestseller *Into the Magic Shop* and founder and director of CCARE at Stanford University School of Medicine.

In this coming-of-age story, a boy who has lost everything walks into the Californian mountains for the very last time. He meets an extraordinary girl with a unique guide to living. She agrees to help him, but first he must overcome many challenges and find answers to some big questions:

- How can he calm his mind?
- Who might change his life forever?
- How can he learn to live with grief?
- Whose love did he crave as a child? Why?
- How can creativity unlock wealth?
- What's hijacking his attention?

All of these questions and more are answered in this simple story about finding love and happiness.

"*Path* is a visual feast!" — Illustrated with thirty beautiful hand sketches of nature and useful diagrams, this book is for everyone still searching for a good life.

Printed in Great Britain
by Amazon

53256720R00098